SAFAR
"Journey"

SAFAR
"Journey"

A Child's Walk
to Freedom During
the Partition of India

Amrik Singh Chattha

Personal History
PRODUCTIONS LLC

From the front cover: "Safar" is an Urdu word that means "journey."

Cover design by Jimmy "Love" Little

ISBN: 978-1721152193

Produced by Personal History Productions LLC

www.personalhistoryproductions.com
United States of America
707.539.5559

In memory of my grandparents,
S. Wadhawa Singh Chattha and Sardarni Ishar Kaur Chattha,
who faced the challenges of Partition with courage and hope.

Also dedicated with love and gratitude to my alma mater,
the Government Medical College, Patiala, in Punjab, India.
She gives all and expects nothing in return.

The past lingers in the present . . .
—Elie Wiesel

Dwell on the past and you'll lose one eye.
Forget the past and you lose both eyes.
—Russian proverb

Contents

Introduction

Though exact figures are impossible to come by, approximately ten to twelve million people were displaced and two hundred thousand to six hundred thousand were killed, abducted, or converted to another religion during the months immediately following the announcement of the Partition of 1947.

Many fine books have been written on this subject, including *Freedom at Midnight,* by Larry Collins and Dominique Lapierre; *Midnight's Furies,* by Nisid Hajari; *The Great Partition,* by Yasmin Khan; *The Punjab Bloodied, Partitioned and Cleansed,* by Ishtiaq Ahmed, and *The Partition of India,* by Ian Talbot and Gurharpal Singh. In addition to these accounts of Partition, some books address specific groups of displaced people, including *The Other Side of Silence,* by Urvashi Butalia, who wrote about the plight of women. According to her, approximately seventy-five thousand women were abducted, raped, killed, disfigured, or forced to convert to another religion. Butalia interviewed many women who were victims of this Punjab holocaust as part of her research. Butalia's focus is on Hindu and Sikh women, but it is important to note that brutality occurred in both countries, Pakistan and India, and was perpetrated by Muslims, Hindus, and Sikhs.

Like Butalia, who was born soon after Partition, many authors of books about Partition were born years later and were not actual participants. Some authors, however, did witness this holocaust, including Kuldip Nayar, Asif Noorani, M. Zahir, V. N. Sekhri, and others.

With many compelling first-person accounts of the upheaval, confusion, violence, depredations, and hardships caused by Partition, why another book? Why another narrative about the effects of Partition on the people of Punjab?

There are three reasons I wrote this account.

First, there are no published first-person, eyewitness accounts of the migration from a Sikh boy's perspective. I was a ten-year-old boy in 1947, and with my family, I experienced the ordeal of life in a *kafla* (caravan) as we were forced to migrate from the western area of Punjab (now Pakistan) to east Punjab (in India). In addition to my *hadd beeti* (personal experience), I share the accounts of two young friends and a cousin.

Second, my hope is that the book might refresh some memories of the older generation, as well as provide historical perspective to the younger generation.

Two books that tell a child's experience of the Jewish Holocaust—Anne Frank's diary and Rutka Laskier's more recently published notebook—have educated and resonated with readers. This book is my attempt to bring to light Sikh children's experiences of Partition. After more than seven decades, very few who suffered as part of the *kaflas* are still around. For the younger generation, it is but a small chapter in history books. We from Punjab need to tell our stories to help us remember and explore the emotional and physical effects of Partition.

My third reason is that as a neurologist, I have had a special interest in the neurobiological and neurochemical basis for the violence that swept an entire continent and destroyed many individuals, families, and communities. In part 6, I examine some factors that contribute to individual and collective religious violence.

Finally, I must apologize for any bias against Islam, which is understandable given the circumstances. I am from the Chattha clan, which has a sizable Muslim population in part of west Punjab, and I have no wish to offend my cousins there. ***Blood is thicker than water.***

Apna hai Phir bhi apna burr kar gale laga le. Acha hai ya bura hey apna use bana ley. (Dear one is dear one, good or bad, just embrace.)

—Mohammed Rafi

India, Late 1947

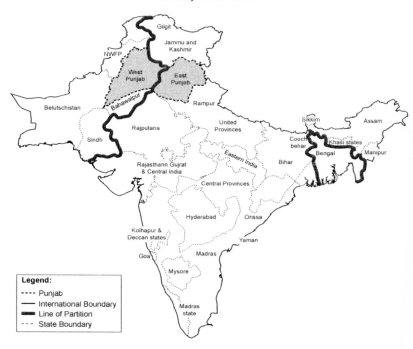

Gilgit

Jammu and
Kashmir

NWFP

West
Punjab

East
Punjab

Rampur

Belutschistan

Bahawalpur

United
Provinces

Sikkim

Assam

Sindh

Rajputana

Cooch
behar

Khasi states

Bengal

Manipur

Rajasthann Gujrat
& Central India

Eastern India

Bihar

Central Provinces

Hyderabad

Orissa

Kolhapur &
Deccan states

Yaman

Goa

Madras

Mysore

Madras
state

Legend:
- - - - Punjab
——— International Boundary
▬▬▬ Line of Partition
- - - State Boundary

Key Locations in Punjab
During Amrik Singh Chattha's Journeys

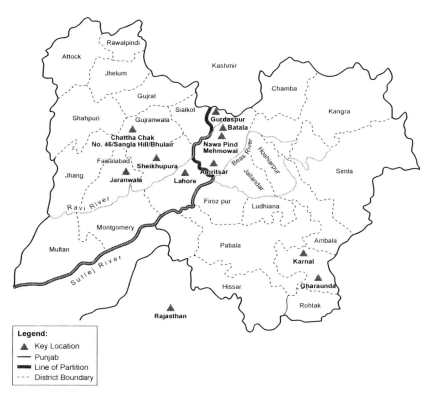

Legend:
▲ Key Location
— Punjab
▩ Line of Partition
--- District Boundary

Part 1

Chatthas in Punjab

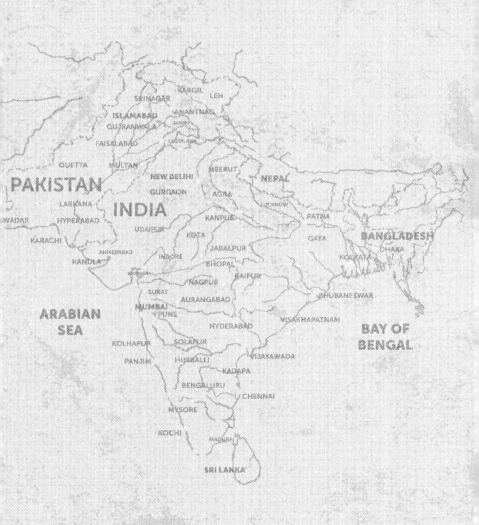

Family

Historically, my family belongs to a subclan of Bhatti Rajputs from what is now Rajasthan, India. At some point many generations ago, they were driven or moved to Punjab. Perhaps they moved because of interclan rivalry or economics. Or perhaps a long drought meant they could not sustain their agriculture and herds of animals. We do not know what caused them to migrate. Regardless, these hunters and gatherers moved with their herds to the lush grazing grounds of Punjab and settled in various places in northern India.

Today, in the district of Gujranwala (located in modern-day Pakistan) there exists a substantial Chattha clan, descendants of my ancestors who migrated from Rajasthan. They are clustered in many villages such as Nikki chatha, Sooianwala chatha, Alipur chatha, Bucha chatha, and Saharan chatha. ("Chatha" or "chattha" loosely translates to "clan of a particular village.") The ancestors of these villagers converted to Islam during the Muslim occupation of Punjab in the thirteenth or fourteenth centuries, when Muslims started moving into Punjab. Meanwhile, members of the clan who settled in other areas of Punjab converted to Sikhism under the influence of Sikh gurus during about the sixteenth century. Still other small Chattha populations exist around Delhi and the state of Haryana, and their ancestors practiced some overlap of Hinduism and Sikhism. They did not wear turbans or keep their hair and did not become Khalsa (baptized Sikhs who follow a certain strict way of living).

My own ancestors, once they reached Punjab, established a small village in the district of Gurdaspur (located in modern-day India) and named it Chattha. The village had both Sikhs and Muslims of the same Chattha lineage who lived peacefully together for many generations. Each group practiced its respective religion and shared each other's joys and sorrows. Belonging to the clan was the thing of most importance.

○   ○   ○

IN THE STORY of my family's experience during the turmoil of Partition, my grandfather, father, and uncle, S. Shingara Singh, were the key figures. Their decisive actions during a dangerous time saved our family.

My Grandfather, S. Wadhawa Singh Chattha

My grandfather, S. Wadhawa Singh, was the middle child. His older brother, S. Nihal Singh, was held in high esteem, which was the cultural norm of rural Punjab Jat Sikh families. (Jats are a clan of Sikh farmers.) The British designated Nihal Singh a *numberdar* (revenue collector) of the village, an honorific title. Land, however, was distributed equally among the three brothers.

My grandfather was born around 1870 in the village of Chattha, located in the district of Gurdaspur, in India. In those days, deliveries were done by a *dhai* (an illiterate village midwife), and no birth

Ancestors and Descendents of Amrik Singh Chattha

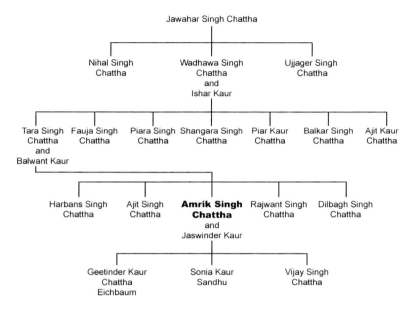

records were kept. When I knew him, he had a deformed right forearm, which could have been congenital or acquired. My cousins and I were curious about it but did not have the courage to ask him. Later, I was told that he broke his arm, and a village orthopedist, a wrestler, bandaged his injured arm too tightly, compromising the blood supply to it and causing his lifelong physical handicap.

Bright and strong willed, my grandfather learned to live and work without the use of his right hand. For instance, he wrote with his left hand and somehow managed to plow the fields. He walked to school in the city of Batala, a six-mile journey each way, and had a eighth-grade education. He could read and write Punjabi as well as Urdu, the official language of the time. Despite his disability, he was able to

Amrik's grandfather's family.

get married to Sardarni Ishar Kaur—this in a time when there was a shortage of females. They had five sons and two daughters. My father, S. Tara Singh, was the oldest child.

My grandfather's strong will and spirit of entrepreneurship pushed him, as a young man, to take advantage of British land development in the western part of Punjab. (Beginning in 1880, the British began turning unsettled land (known as *barr*) in arid west Punjab into land more suitable for agriculture using a series of canals for large-scale irrigation. The villages and towns that grew up from this development were known as "canal colonies.") So along with his brothers and other members of his original Chattha village (as well as non-clan Sikhs and Muslims in support occupations), he moved west in the early 1900s from Gurdaspur to newly developed land in an area called Barr, which is now part of modern-day Pakistan.

There they established a new village, called Chattha Chak No. 46. The land of the new *chak* (village) was flat, and irrigation came from a network of canals. There was enough land for many villagers to own their own acreage.

My grandfather and his two brothers later divided land among themselves and had separate homes. Once in a while, my grandfather and his brothers leased part of their land to other people, which provided an additional source of income for our family.

Like their original Chattha village, this Chattha village was a self-sufficient unit. However, *unlike* the first Chattha village, the Sikhs and the Muslims in this village lived separately. The physical distance allowed each group to practice its own religion. For instance, Muslims could sacrifice cows in their area, and Sikhs could slaughter pigs. Each group also had separate places for worship: Sikhs had a Gurdwara and a Granthi (preacher), while Muslims had a mosque and a mullah. They did, however, have a common school.

Despite their differences, Sikh Chatthas and Muslim Chatthas were still kin, and they interacted with each other. For instance, I remember attending the Muslim marriage ceremony of my distant uncle Jallaludin's daughter.

Farmers like my grandfather often went to Sangla Hill, a town a mile and a half from Chak No. 46, for business and pleasure. Each month in Sangla Hill there was an auction of cows, bullocks, water buffaloes, and other domestic animals. And twice a year, after harvest, farmers took their produce, loaded onto wagons, there to sell. At these events, my grandfather socialized with his buddies—both Sikh and Muslim.

My grandfather's friends included Jamadar Sher Mohammed and an elderly hunchback potter whom he had known his whole life, even back in their old Chattha village. Both Muslim men visited frequently.

As a sign of respect, everyone in the village addressed my grandfather as *Sardar Sahib* (respected man). The only man who addressed my grandfather by his first name was his friend Sher Mohammed. Grandfather was also visited frequently by some of his Muslim farm tenants. The visits were both business and social.

Villagers in rural Punjab in those days were very litigious regarding land and water rights. My grandfather was no exception and even kept attorneys on retainer at district headquarters. Over the years, he developed friendships with them. The attorneys sometimes even provided night accommodations if he missed the only train running from district headquarters to Sangla Hill, the railway station closest to our village.

It was in this village, Chattha Chak No. 46, where I was born in 1937. I was raised in an extended family, with many cousins, presided over by my grandfather.

In today's society, it is often mothers who encourage and oversee education and performance; however, in old rural Punjab, these were the purview of fathers and grandfathers. (In old Punjab, mothers did not have career-building roles in their children's lives; instead, their roles were to cook and bear and care for children. They were, however, advisors to their daughters and taught them cooking, sewing, and other skills to prepare them to be wives and mothers. There were no other career choices for girls.)

My grandfather certainly valued education, and school grades determined whom he favored among his grandchildren. Higher grades in school meant you could have extra milk and would be showered with his praise in the presence of family members and visitors. Still, while my grandfather encouraged education and rewarded good grades, he did not punish poor performance. In fact, he would show interest in all his grandchildren by visiting our schools two or three times a year and inquiring about our performance.

Overall, though, my grandfather's interaction with his grandchildren was limited. I was therefore surprised when, one evening, my grandfather—whom I called "Bapu ji"—pulled me aside to ask what I had learned that day in school. Since we had been studying idioms as part of our English-language lesson, I told him about the idiom "An excess of everything is bad." He was surprised and said, "What is bad about having too much wheat or cotton?" He became curious and asked me the next day about anything else I had learned. I told him about the idiom "When in Rome do as the Romans do." He laughed and said, "I will do what I want to do. I don't want to copy others." His answer may have been concrete, but it was also practical. He was a confident and independent thinker. Given the illiteracy prevalent in Punjab in those days, he and his sons were considered quite smart, so much so that one of his visiting friends jokingly asked, *"Wadhawa Singh, sanu thora apna bee dey dey?"* (Can you give us some of your genes?)

My grandfather continued to contribute to the advancement of our family, even well into an advanced age.

During his lifetime, many of his grandchildren excelled—for instance, one entered medicine, one the law, and one civil service—and moved to urban areas. My grandfather could not quite believe this. He had grown up during a time in old Punjab when men mostly worked on family farms and, if they got some education, might be able to join the army, police, or civil service as *patwaris* (land record officers and revenue collectors). More desirable jobs—such as those in the Indian Civil Service (ICS), engineering, medicine, and the law—were within reach of only elite families with British connections. That he had grandchildren who were successful in these fields surprised him.

As he aged, my grandfather became more mellow. For most of his life, he had been pro-British—in fact, he raised horses for the

British cavalry—and had no liking for Gandhi, Nehru, Jinnah, and even the Sikh political party, Akali Dal. He was doubtful that Indian independence, championed by these leaders, would be good for the people. He feared that freedom could lead to ruin. Though he never used the phrase himself, the slogan *"azadi* is *barbadi"* (freedom leads to destruction) was frequently in the press, and when I think of my grandfather in his earlier years, that phrase summed up his feelings. Over time, however, his feelings changed, and as an older man, he spoke out less against Indian leaders.

My grandfather and his two brothers died in their seventies. My grandmother died of old age and Alzheimer's disease.

My Father, Tara Singh Chattha

My father, Tara Singh Chattha, was born around 1910 in Chak No. 46. He went to primary school in the village and then attended high school in the nearby town of Sangla Hill. Two of his brothers followed the same educational path, and all three graduated from high school—a rare accomplishment for that time and place. My father was bright, kind, and loving. He and my mother, Sardarni Balwant Kaur, married in their early teens and eventually had five sons. I am the middle child.

My father spent two years at Khalsa College Amritsar, the premier Sikh institution of the time. Because his family could not afford to send more than one son to college, my father was the only one among his siblings to receive any college education. Because of the Great Depression and the resulting worldwide economic malaise, he could not continue his studies in liberal arts. After his second year of college, he was recruited by and joined the British Army. For a while during World War II, he was on the Burmese front. When the British left, he chose to make a career as a noncommissioned officer in the army with its slow promotion path instead of opting for temporary officer commission, which, though more prestigious and better paying, was not secure. His brother, S. Shingara Singh, ten years younger, also chose to become a noncommissioned officer in the army. Their brothers Fauja Singh, Piara Singh, and Balkar Singh stayed home to supervise the farm and care for the animals.

Although my father's and uncle's positions provided steady jobs and salaries, giving our family a measure of economic stability not enjoyed by villagers who farmed or otherwise relied on the village economy, they were away in the army for most of my growing-up years. They had vacation only once a year for about two months, so that's about the only time we saw my father and uncle. In their absence, our extended family of aunts, uncles, and cousins was presided over by my grandfather, who made all decisions concerning our education, the farm, and finances.

My father retired in 1960, after thirty-five years of service, about the time I graduated from medical school. By that point, one of my brothers was already an engineer, and another was studying engineering in college. My father retired as an honorary lieutenant (an honorary title given to a retiree) and had a fulfilling postretirement life till the death of my oldest brother, S. Harbans Singh, in 1969. After my brother's death, my father took on the responsibility of raising Harbans's four children, guiding them and making education and marriage decisions. My father died in an auto accident in his mid-seventies.

My grandfather and father differed in one important regard: my grandfather was pro-British, while my father was for freedom. (I never heard my mother express her views.) My grandfather raised horses for the British cavalry and saw the order and relative peace the British imposed on the subcontinent as a necessary and overall good thing. My father, meanwhile, an educated man, worked under the British. In a sense, they were his masters. He longed for an India ruled by Indians for Indians. He understood the virtues of freedom.

My Mother, Sardarni Balwant Kaur

My mother, Balwant Kaur, was born about 1910 in the village of Gill, about two miles from our village of Chak No. 46. She was the niece of my grandfather's close friend and was about the same age as my father. My parents' marriage was, of course, arranged. My mother never had the opportunity to attend school. After she married, she raised five sons and also four grandchildren (Harbans's four children, after his death), as well as many of her sister's children. Her sister lived in a faraway village with no school, so she sent her children to my mother during the school year so they could attend school.

Growing up, I never saw my parents angry, anxious, or depressed. They were kind and charitable people.

My Childhood

My memories as a young child are happy ones. I had a loving, large extended family with cousins of the same age. As toddlers, we would roam around diaperless, wearing a long shirt (made from homespun Kaddhar cloth) that went to our knees. I was favorite of my *bhuas* (paternal aunts), who played with me and carried me around. Our toys were mostly made of wood or clay. When we got a little older, we played group games like hide-and-seek, marbles, hockey, and cards. For breakfast, we usually ate *roti* (bread), milk, yogurt, and butter. For regular meals we ate lot of *dal* (lentils), *sag* (greens), and rice. Cooking was done in *chulhas* (traditional earthen stoves) that would be kept lit all night to avoid the need to start a new fire in the morning. When we had visitors, we might get to eat meat. We all went to seasonal *melas* (festivals) like Vaisakhi, Diwali, and Basant, and I looked forward to going to the Gurdwara (Sikh place of worship) every month especially to enjoy *prashad* (a sweet pudding) served at the end. All my friends were Sikh; unlike my grandfather, I did not have any Muslim friends.

I began school at the age of four, carrying my *basta* (school bag), *bori* (jute mat), *phatti* (a wooden plank plastered with clay on which we could write and then wash clean), ink pot, and pen (made of cane). I had a hard time waking up each morning, so my mother regularly rousted me by shouting, "Get up!" (There was no clock in the house, so they estimated time from the whistle of the morning train.) Primary school was in the Muslim area of Chak No. 46, within walking distance of my house. The school had two rooms, but classes were often conducted outside, under the shade of a tree. The teacher was a Hindu from nearby Sangla Hill. I remember that he had a shortened Achilles tendon on his right foot from polio, a condition that forced him to walk on his toes on his right foot. Children being children, we nicknamed him Master Addi Chuck, which translates to "Mr. Lift-One-Heel." The teacher was a tough and unkind man who kept order in the school through corporal punishment, including caning.

I was a good student who escaped punishment from Master Addi Chuck, but I experienced harassment from some other students who didn't like me because I was a class monitor and teacher's assistant. They would try to knock off my turban, a sign of disrespect. When my older brothers or cousins were around, they would keep the bullies away.

My father was away in the Indian Army, and my mother was busy in kitchen, so my activities were watched over by my older brothers, my grandfather, and, during school hours, the schoolteacher. At age ten, my life changed. From then on, I would attend school in various locations in India.

Animosity Rises in the Villages

L ife in general in Chattha Chak No. 46 was peaceful, but for many, many years, there had been subtle—and sometimes pronounced— enmity and distrust between Muslims and their Sikh neighbors. The animosity was widespread—nearly universal in India—because Islam was seen by Hindus and Sikhs as an "outside" religion that had, to some extent, been forced on the existing Hindu population centuries ago.

In the twentieth century, the animosity gradually increased as the Muslim League agitated for a separate homeland for Muslims. In our village of Chak No. 46, however, at least on the surface, mutual respect between Muslim and Sikh members of the Chattha clan persisted, for a while.

As it became more apparent from 1945 to 1947 that the British planned to leave India, unrest in Punjab became more pronounced. Though the men and women in Chak No. 46 and surrounding villages were mostly illiterate, they were still somewhat aware of politics— because politics was so intricately tied to religion in India.

In Punjab, there were four primary political parties:

o Akali Dal (mostly Sikhs)
o Muslim League (mostly Muslims)
o Indian National Congress (secular and mostly non-Muslims)
o Nonpolitical

Most Sikhs were part of Akali Dal, a political party that called for a Sikh-majority state in Punjab. Akali Dal grew out of an earlier Akali movement, which sought to have Gurdwaras freed from the control of British-appointed *mahants* (hereditary managers of Gurdwaras). Sikhs raised their voice against the idea of Pakistan, which would envelop the part of India where most Sikhs lived.

The Muslim League, meanwhile, wanted separate a Muslim-majority area, to be called Pakistan.

Till the end, the Congress was against a division of India. Other individuals were for the status quo and against freedom for India. My grandfather was one of them. He had over the years developed good relations with British officers and wanted no part of freedom. For him *"azadi* was *barbadi"* (freedom brings ruin). He was right for a while, as evidenced by the violence and destruction that followed freedom in 1947.

Part 2

The Lead-up to Partition

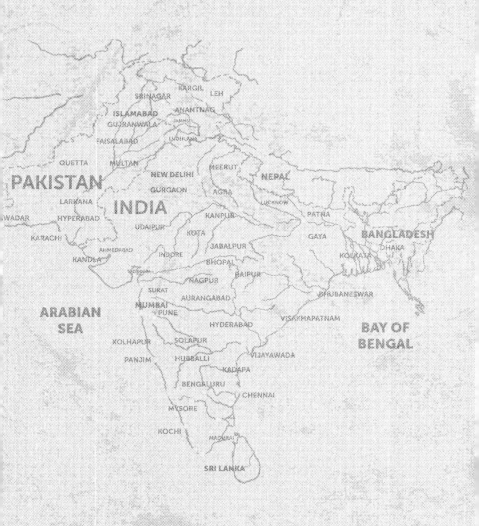

First Encounter with the British

As a boy, I had no idea about slavery, even though we were a slave nation under the British Raj. The rulers had the power to promote their loyal subjects. For instance, my grandfather was pro-British and got favors from local British officers, including *korrie da murabba* (additional land to raise horses) for their cavalry. And his older brother, also pro-British, was nominated as a local village head (*lambardar*) and collected land tax for the Raj. Also, through my grandfather's connections with a British district deputy commissioner (as well as a letter of recommendation from my father's college president), my father and uncle were made noncommissioned officers in the army. These were some of the perks of being pro-British-rule.

When I was about eight years old, my grandfather turned his attention to the careers of his grandsons. Good jobs often relied on connections with British authorities, and my grandfather had cultivated some goodwill with them through his work breeding and raising horses for them. So one wintery morning, my grandfather took my older brother S. Ajit Singh and me to the local railway station to take the train to Sheikhupur, the district headquarters. My grandfather planned to introduce us to Mr. Hunter, the district deputy commissioner who had secured a spot in the army for my father. There was no system of scheduling appointments, so we hoped that Mr. Hunter would be in his office that morning.

As we three stood in front of his office, a middle-aged man of medium height wearing a khaki uniform came out. He wore a top hat and had a bamboo stick tucked under his right arm. He waved his stick and addressed my grandfather, apparently remembering his name. He asked in half-broken Urdu, "Wadhawa Singh, what brings you here?"

"Sahib," said my grandfather, "here are my two grandchildren, sons of Tara Singh, my son, whom you helped get enlisted in the British Army. I want you to kindly keep in mind army jobs for them when they grow up."

Mr. Hunter said, "Wow! They are *kakkey*" (fair-colored). He must have been impressed with a light complexion in a Punjabi family. He advised my grandfather to send us to college and said he would help us enroll as officers. Mr. Hunter probably had no inkling that the British Raj was close to its end.

Our meeting lasted only about five minutes, and we then headed back to our village. My grandfather was happy that his mission was accomplished. He had started the ball rolling for our future. My brother and I couldn't have cared less and thought it was just a formality. This speaks to my grandfather's PR skills and his concern for the future of his grandchildren. (As it turned out, I never saw Mr. Hunter again.)

ABOUT FIFTY YEARS after I relocated to America, I attended a medical meeting in Scotland with a few physician colleagues and had dinner and drinks at Dalhousie Castle, the former home of the man who had been governor-general of India from 1848 to 1856. We were greeted, as is tradition, by a band of kilt-wearing bagpipers. A trip to his castle reminded me of a trip my father had made to Simla Hills, the summer capital of Punjab during the Raj. During the British Raj, there were signs on the mall saying "Dogs and Indians Not Allowed."

As I stood in the home of the former ruler of India, I thought, "What a change!

I hate Indians. They are a beastly people . . .

—Winston Churchill, 1943

The British after World War II

After World War II ended, in 1945, the British were in no mood to hold on to their colonies. World War II had taken a heavy toll on the British population and its treasury. Churchill had been keen to keep British colonies, but he lost the 1945 general election, and the new leadership stood ready to dismantle its empire. Local agitations and revolts against the Raj were brewing, and the new prime minister, Clement Attlee, feared Britain was losing the loyalty of the Indian Armed Services. The British were in a hurry to leave India. As the saying goes, "Hurry makes bad curry"; so were the consequences of hurried partition. Lord Mountbatten, the last viceroy, was sent to hand India over to its representatives.

The Indian National Congress—led by Jawaharlal Nehru, Vallabhbhai Patel, Maulana Azad, and Gandhi—wanted a united country, while the Muslim League, headed by Muhammad Ali Jinnah, wanted a separate country with a Muslim-majority population. Jinnah was adamant for partition. At one time, he had been a supporter of an undivided India and was considered an ambassador for Hindu-Muslim unity. But he blamed Gandhi for mixing religion with politics and began to advocate for a new state of Pakistan, with a Muslim majority, created from parts of India.

It was a seeming impasse. After negotiation, all parties agreed to subdivide India, splitting Punjab and Bengal into West Pakistan and East Pakistan, respectively. No decision was made for the princely states. (The princely states were small kingdoms spread throughout India. They were mostly independent, with limited involvement from the British Raj.) The princely states were finally integrated in Pakistan or India, except for Kashmir. This state had a Hindu Raja ruling a Muslim-majority population and was also was geographically located between the two new nations. Tensions over Kashmir continue to this day.

A retired judge, Cyril Radcliffe, came from England to India to divide the country along religious lines. It was not possible to have a Muslim-dominated country surrounded by a majority of Hindus; therefore, Radcliffe took a practical view and used the periphery of the country. Both Punjab and Bengal were knifed to make West Pakistan and East Pakistan. Because the two portions lay many miles apart, they could not be integrated into one single country; there were also cultural and linguistic differences in the two regions. Now the two are separate countries: Pakistan on the west and Bangladesh on the east.

....

The jewel in the crown is shattered.

....

Information, Media, and Partition

In 1947, people in Punjab villages had no newspaper, telephone, radio, TV, or social media. And even if they had had newspapers, most of them could not read the news. Word traveled from village to village mostly by word of mouth. Sometimes the delay or lack of information was a blessing. For example, news of the violence that roiled India in the lead-up to Partition was delayed in reaching Punjab villages such as our village, Chak No. 46. We did not learn of the violence in Bengal, for instance, until two weeks after it occurred.

Only leaders in New Delhi who had meetings with Lord Mountbatten had some idea of what was to come. The common folk, meanwhile, were receiving no information or incorrect information, and as a result, the people in Punjab most affected by British decisions and Indian political machinations—villagers up and down the line of Partition, on both sides—were not prepared to undertake a migration. Even Sikh leaders such as Master Tara Singh and Baldev Singh were not sure of the boundary line.

None of the leaders—of any party—completely anticipated the ultimate consequence of the birth of Pakistan: the violence that overtook Punjab.

24

Independence and I

At my young age, I did not understand the meaning of independence or freedom.

The Sikh population in Punjab first heard talk of Partition, and the possibility of the creation of a Muslim country, in their Gurdwaras. Maybe they took independence for granted; after all, who could imagine what was to come?

I remember first hearing about this approximately two years before Partition. Some older cousins took me along to a conference for freedom held at Sangla Hill. I recall that lectures were given and poems recited. I could not have cared less about the lectures, but two poems by anonymous authors still ring in my mind. These were addressed to the British and delivered by a poet with a Virk tribe dialect: *"Thune sathi, birle, Tate da dalmiae te bate da sanu buk nei milda ate da."* (You are friends to Birla, Tata, Dalmia, and Bata [big business houses], but we do not get even a handful of flour.) The second poem then rang out: *"As Angrezan de kute te khan de ne biscuit te sadian nu nei milda toda."* (The dogs of the British eat biscuits while ours do not get halfbaked thick bread.) These poems expressed outrage over an economic recession and the rationing of daily necessities, such as wheat, rice, sugar, and kerosene. Both the recession and the rationing aggravated Indians' anti-British stance. Indians wanted independence. They wanted to control their own destiny, not have a foreign master.

Personally, I did not know what slavery was till my grandfather took my brother and me to meet Mr. Hunter, the district deputy commissioner, a few months later. At that meeting, I was surprised to notice that my grandfather was intimidated by this man. It was then that I recognized that my grandfather thought Mr. Hunter had authority over him.

By early 1947, when I was a young boy of ten, I had grasped the concept of both independence and slavery. The reality of Pakistan and Partition sank in a few months later; however, at the time I had no anxiety or panic. Maybe my calmness was because I had the stable base of a caring family.

Sikhs and Independence

Sikhs had always taken a very active part in the struggle for freedom from the British. Young revolutionaries—men like S. Bhagat Singh and Udham Singh—were revered heroes. Many Sikhs had been slaughtered by the British Indian Army at the Jallianwala Bagh massacre, in Amritsar, in 1919, as the crowd nonviolently protested the British Raj.

Sikhs were represented by the political party Akali Dal, which was led by Master Tara Singh, S. Baldev Singh, Giani Kartar Singh, Harnam Singh, and Maharaja Yadvinder Singh of Patiala. Akali Dal later developed an alliance with the All India Congress.

The British were sympathetic to Sikh demands, even though Sikhs constituted only a small fraction of the population. They were scattered all over Punjab, and because there was no Sikh majority in any significant geographical location, their demand for a three-way split of India—Hindu, Muslim, Sikh—was destined to fail. Most Sikh religious shrines were in Punjab, so the idea of Sikhs being part of Pakistan or losing Punjab to Pakistan was a nightmare for them.

The political rhetoric ramped up on all sides. For instance, slogans in support of Pakistan—*zindabad Mr. Jinnah!* (long live Mr. Jinnah!)—began appearing in public places. Sikh leader Master Tara Singh waved his *kirpan* (dagger) in front of the Punjab legislative assembly building in Lahore, the capital of Punjab, yelling that Punjab would be divided "over my dead body."

These events were discussed and disseminated in monthly Sikh assemblies in Gurdwaras. Even we children knew about them. All this became very scary and made my grandfather nervous. *Azadi is barbadi.* Freedom is a dangerous game. The everyday news was worse: violence was spreading among religious groups. What should Sikh farmers do? Should they leave everything behind and head to India? Or fight to the death? A neighboring village of ours, called Bhulair, opted for the latter.

Sikh Demands

Sikhs constituted just a fraction of the population of India, but central Punjab was inhabited by Sikh farmers, many of whom were financially well off. Despite this, the British boundary commission did not give any consideration to Sikhs and their demands, even though they were sympathetic to the Sikhs because of their military contribution during World War II. (They had been a major part of the British Indian Army.)

Sikh leaders like Master Tara Singh and S. Baldev Singh pleaded that the Indo-Pak line of demarcation should be at the level of the Chenab River. If the boundary had been drawn at the Chenab, most of the Sikh shrines would have remained part of India. Sikhs would also have gotten a larger portion of Punjab. The boundary commission, however, put the line of demarcation at the level of the Ravi River, which meant that central Punjab and many Sikh shrines would be in Pakistan.

Of course, Sikhs in the part of Punjab that was now west of the line of partition did not want to be part of Pakistan. However, they were reluctant to leave their land, homes, and religious shrines. This frustration was partially responsible for formation of Sikh *jathas* (militias).

Some Sikhs held out hope that a Sikh empire could be re-created in Punjab with the help of Sikh princely states, which had ruled Punjab before British annexation. Sikh leaders in 1946 had meetings with Jinnah, who tried every olive branch to woo Sikhs to avoid the partition of Punjab. Although nothing was put in writing, Jinnah promised Sikhs that they could remain, unharmed, in Punjab, though they would be treated as a minority. He said they could maintain their shrines. These meetings failed due to historical mistrust. Would subsequent leaders of Pakistan honor Jinnah's promises to the Sikhs? In view of subsequent events in Pakistan, Sikhs made the right decision. It could be, however, that if Sikhs had stayed in west Punjab, as a powerful minority they might have changed the direction of Pakistan. We will never know.

Malcolm Darling

Malcolm Darling was a British citizen, a former Indian Civil Service (ICS) officer who had served in Punjab and had a special interest in the citizens of that area. In 1925, he published a book titled *The Punjab Peasant in Prosperity and Debt*. After his retirement to England, he returned to northern India once again, at the end of 1946, with his daughter and son-in-law, and together they traveled on horseback through much of India, beginning in Peshawar. Darling's aim was to learn what villagers were thinking and how they had been affected by World War II. The timing of his trip is significant, however, coming as it did on the cusp of independence and partition; his reports are a window into the understanding and thinking of Punjabi villagers in that time of uncertainty.

As the three travelers rode through Punjab, Darling visited villages and asked farmers—many of them Muslim—what they thought about the idea of Pakistan. He wanted to learn how Punjabis perceived independence. According to his diary, most Punjabis did not know much about Pakistan and what the future held for them. Most Muslims, when asked about Jinnah, answered that Jinnah would save them from Hindus. (This answer was probably less about the Hindu religion and more about Hindu money lenders, like Blaki Mall, who was the largest nonbank lender in Lahore [Ahmed].) When Darling asked a young Sikh his thoughts, however, the young man replied, "*Azadi* is *barbadi*" (freedom is destruction) and "Pakistan is *kabaristan*" (a graveyard). Many villagers whom Darling interviewed asked for the British to stay for a time, while others complained about the rationing of sugar and fabric imposed by the British.

Everybody, however, wanted independence.

Around December 20, 1946, Mr. Darling's party reached Sangla Hill, the place where I went to school through fifth grade and only two miles from my village, Chattha Chak No. 46.

Here Darling met the elderly Sikh Maharaj Singh, who was chairman of my school board as well as manager of a local bank. My grandfather was a member of the school board, and I am sure he knew Maharaj Singh.

Maharaj Singh had a long discussion with Darling and emphasized impending communal riots over the partition of Punjab. Had Darling been able to share villagers' concerns with British authorities, perhaps they might have made different decisions. Maybe bloodshed could have been avoided or reduced if British authorities had gotten feedback from the grassroots level. Both the Indian Congress and the Muslim League were aware of riots that had occurred earlier in Calcutta (now Kolkata); maybe they thought bloodshed was the unavoidable price for independence. This sentiment was verbalized by H. S. Suhrawardy, then chief minister of Bengal, when he said, "Bloodshed and disorder are not necessarily evil in themselves if resorted to for a noble cause." In any case, Darling had been retired from service for quite some time and had no channel to British decision makers.

Mr. Darling continued his journey through the rest of Punjab and on to Jabalpur. His experience and discourses with villagers are found in his book *At Freedom's Door.*

The Concept of Pakistan

The idea of a Muslim state or country was conceived by Choudhry Rahmat Ali (a Muslim Punjabi founder in 1932 of the Pakistan National Movement, who is credited with creating the name "Pakistan"), nurtured by Allama Iqbal (a politician and poet), and completed by Muhammad Ali Jinnah. All three men had studied abroad and had knowledge of Zionism and knew of the writings of Theodor Herzl and his advocacy of a Jewish homeland, which influenced their thinking. Their idea was to carve a Muslim-majority area in India into a sovereign state, free from Hindu dominance, so that Muslims could have political and religious freedom. The areas under consideration included Punjab, Afghanistan, Kashmir, Sindh, and Balochistan. The leaders of the movement stated that other religious groups, such as Hindus, Sikhs, and Christians, could stay as minorities. Their argument had some practical flaws, for instance:

○ Why would Hindus and Sikhs agree to live as minorities in Pakistan when there was long-standing hatred among these communities?

- Most towns and villages in eastern Punjab had a Hindu and Sikh majority; hence all of Punjab could not be part of a Muslim Pakistan.
- Could the area under consideration sustain all Indian Muslims?
- Except for religion, there was no cultural or linguistic bond between Muslim-majority western Punjab and Bengal, and the two areas were approximately 1,000 miles apart. (Choudhry Rahmat Ali had recognized this fact and had not included Bengal in his idea of Pakistan.)
- Afghanistan was a sovereign country and therefore could not legally be considered.

After World War II, with independence from the British almost guaranteed, there was wind behind the Muslim League and the idea of creating Pakistan. Any Muslim against this idea was considered a traitor. For example, Maulana Abul Kalam Azad, a Muslim Congress member against the creation of Pakistan, was not liked by League leaders. (He ultimately opted to stay in free India, never moving to Pakistan.)

Warning voices such as Azad's were muffled. Peer pressure and herd mentality took over. Even if leaders had wanted to rethink the arrangement, the genie could not be put back in bottle. Many think even Jinnah was ambivalent about the idea of Pakistan, but it was too late. The costs to the common Punjabi—displacement, human misery, and loss of life—were ignored by the leaders. Also ignored were the extreme economic hardships many Indians would face because of the upheaval. Malcolm Darling, the old Englishman, had gotten this message when he traveled through Punjab just prior to independence.

THE MAIN POLITICAL leaders involved in independence and partition at this time were as follows:

Great Britain

>Clement Attlee, Prime Minister
>Louis Mountbatten, Viceroy of India

India

Indian National Congress

>Mahatma Gandhi
>Jawaharlal Nehru
>Vallabhbhai Patel
>Abul Kalam Azad

Akali Dal

>Master Tara Singh
>Giani Kartar Singh
>Baldev Singh

Muslim League

>Muhammad Ali Jinnah
>Liaquat Ali Khan

Muhammad Ali Jinnah

Liaquat Ali Khan

Group shot of Mountbatten with Indian leaders.

Master Tara Singh   *Jawaharlal Nehru and Gandhi*

Sardar Vallabhbhai Patel   *Maulana Abul Kalam Azad*   *Clement Attlee*

Baldev Singh   *Giani Kartar Singh*

IT IS SAD TO SAY, but the aspiration and excitement of most of these leaders were different from the worries and anxieties of the population at large, which had more to lose. All the leaders of various political parties were quite rich, and most had studied abroad. Further, most had no contact with or feel for India's poor and its farmers. The minds of most leaders were focused on freedom at any cost.

There were exceptions, such as Gandhi and the Akali leaders. I have personally met Akali leader Giani Kartar Singh. As a legislator, he lived in a humble dwelling at Chandigarh along with three other *jathedars* (Sikh regional leaders). I did not see any bodyguards around him. Similarly, Master Tara Singh was a devout Sikh and served his community. Their descendants, unlike those of the other leaders, did not indulge in politics and material gains.

While I have great regard for leaders of those days, these men had limited political experience. The argument could be made that they were amateurs. Still, for anyone it would have been challenging to deal with a large country plagued by poverty and illiteracy and with a diversity of language, religion, and culture. The leaders worked hard and experienced jail time—but none experienced loss of life or property. (Later, after Partition, both Gandhi and Liaquat Ali Khan were assassinated.) Most were rewarded with political careers, which became dynastic.

While the leaders mentioned above are the ones whose names are in the history books, regular villagers—people whose names are remembered only by family and friends—also did their part for freedom. They displayed quiet leadership and sacrifice and took part in agitations. For instance, my uncle Fauja Singh took part in many anti-British agitations, which twice landed him in jail. His last *morcha* (agitation) was at the town of Jaito. He took part in these *morchas* against wishes of my grandfather, who jokingly commented that my uncle went to jail to avoid hard life at the family farm. In his old age, my uncle was given the status of freedom fighter, which came with a pension and the privilege of free first-class travel on Indian railway with one relative or attendant. He enjoyed this only for a brief period before his death. My uncle rightly deserves his photograph along with other leaders in the pages of this book.

Partition

A well-established strategy used by invading forces for thousands of years is known as "divide and rule." A divide and rule policy breaks up large concentrations of power into weaker ones that oppose each other, thus helping a conqueror gain and maintain power. This strategy was successfully used by Assyrians to conquer Babylon and Syria, by Romans to conquer Gaul, and, in recent history, by the British for control of its colonies.

In India, the British "divided" by such tactics as establishing boundaries for different religions and establishing quotas for each religious group in professions and in organizations such as the Indian army, which had regiments of religious groups. While the British had a soft spot for Sikhs because of their notable military service and courage, politically, the British favored Muslims because the Muslim League supported them during the World War II. Some people even theorized that the British favored Muslims because both Christianity and Islam trace their lineages to Abraham, while Christianity and Hinduism have no historic commonality.

"Divide and rule" worked well till Indians became enlightened.

Also, World War II had a devastating effect on Great Britain. Leaving India peacefully was urgent. Divide and rule had no meaning at this moment in history. Sir Penderel Moon, a member of the ICS, wrote *Divide and Quit,* describing events of 1947. In the book, he suggests that the British, in fact, genuinely wanted an undivided free India. Lady Ethel Manners, the widow of a former governor in Paul Scott's 1966 novel *The Jewel in the Crown*, lamented, "The creation of Pakistan is our crowning failure. I can't bear it. . . . Our only justification for two hundred years of power was unification. But we've divided one composite nation into two and everyone at home goes round saying what a swell the new Viceroy is for getting it sorted out so quickly." Though fiction, the sentiments were accurate.

There were distinct advantages in having a large, undivided India:

○ The trauma of partition could have been avoided.
○ People would have continued, unfettered access to their religious places.
○ Kashmir, with its related defense expense and terrorism, would not be an issue.
○ A larger India might not have been bullied by its neighbors, especially China.
○ The superpowers might have kept their hands off. (Russia might not have invaded Afghanistan, in 1979, because an undivided India may not have tolerated a communist country at its border.)
○ Al Qaeda and ISIS might not have been born.
○ Some of the expense for defense could have been diverted to benefit the society.
○ India might have learned to live with its religious diversity, like Malaysia, South Africa, and Ireland ultimately have.

The above scenario, however, appears too rosy. An undivided India would have been in constant religious conflict, sapping resources with a failed democracy and possibly military rule. What would have been the fate of undivided India is anybody's guess. Gandhi and Maulana Abul Kalam Azad were the only national leaders advocating for undivided India. (See Winners and Losers, page 167, for more discussion.)

My grandfather and my friend Ajit Singh Chattha both were in favor of undivided Punjab. If I told my grandfather that I learned a new idiom in school, "United we stand, divided we fall," I am sure he would have approved. He was convinced about freedom but still against the division of Punjab.

The Creation of Pakistan

On August 14, 1947, Pakistan became a reality.

Nobody would be happier about the creation of the new country than Bhai Parmanand of Hindu Mahasabha (a political party), who had been first to advocate in 1909 that Muslims should be isolated to northwest India. Sardar Vallabhbhai Patel, leader of the Indian National Congress party, was happy the "diseased limb" was being removed; in other words, that Muslims were being corralled in Pakistan.

The Muslim League got, as Jinnah later described Pakistan, "a moth-eaten" and smaller country. They thought the British betrayed them by not giving them a consolidated country but instead East Pakistan and West Pakistan. However, in the end, Muslim leaders and rich and educated Muslims got what they wished for, leaving behind a Hindu-dominated India with a poorer Muslim minority.

The British exited India in a hurry. "Now or never" won, while "wait and watch" lost. ("Now or never" was a phrase coined by Choudhary Rahmat Ali.) British leaders did not think a slow, measured withdrawal was in its self-interest.

Compare the creation of Israel to the creation of Pakistan: It took many years of discussion and deliberation before the Jewish state was established, while the Muslim League had very little time to put in place systems to handle law and order, migrants, rehabilitation, and so forth. Most important, they did not establish a workable democracy. Still, careful, slow deliberation is no guarantee of success. Homelands such as Israel, built on religious grounds, are in constant conflict with others. (Decades ago, the Khalistan movement advocated the creation of a Sikh-majority homeland, to be located mostly in east Punjab. I am glad many Sikhs opposed this movement.)

NOW OR NEVER
Are we to live or perish for ever?
—Rahmat Ali Choudhary and others, 1933

Villages

Village folk had some idea about partition and the creation of Pakistan. They had heard rumors about violence against Hindus and Sikhs in northwest Punjab and Bengal. But overall, they were in the dark. Newspapers had stopped printing, and villagers did not have access to radio.

Jinnah and the congress leadership did not anticipate any religious cleansing or migration of population. In fact, both parties wanted to protect minorities in their respective newly formed countries. Lord Mountbatten also did not anticipate violence.

The talk among party leaders was markedly different from the talk at the local level. Among Sikh farmers and leaders, concern centered on such immediate things as their livelihood, family, animals, and homes. What did it all mean for them, who had lived for generations on the land? For instance, my distant uncle Ram Singh was adamant that he would rather die than leave his home. He spoke the thoughts of many.

Despite exaggerated reports of violence against Sikhs and Muslims delivered to the villagers of Chak No. 46 from the Gurdwara and the mosque, our village remained calm. Even after we heard the report of the boundary commission, peace prevailed. Why? Mostly likely the calm in our village—though short-lived—was due to a common Chattha lineage and a shared profession as farmers.

The village even had a saying: *Chattha te Cheeme Khan nu ado ad lurrand nu kathe.* (Clan of Chattha and Cheema may live and eat separately, but get together if they have to battle and fight.)

Over a period of a few months, however, hatred had built between religions in our village. As a child, I noticed that Muslim friends of my grandfather stopped visiting him. And the attitude that poorer sections of Muslim society had toward Sikhs was outright hatefulness and disrespect. I clearly remember the glares and menacing body language of the Muslim boys in the village toward us Sikh boys. They and their families were hoping we would leave so they could possess our homes, land, and animals—which they later did.

Our village had about ten Christians families who provided services for Sikh families. Though poor, they played very positive and loyal roles during the time of turmoil. For instance, they delivered messages from one Sikh village to another, wearing red crosses on their chest, a sign that afforded them safe passage. Two loyal Christian employees of my distant uncle Man Singh's family accompanied his family during the migration all the way to India; they went back the moment Uncle's family was settled in east Punjab. Similarly, one loyal employee stayed in India with my friend Dr. Bhullar's uncle's family for one year after Partition.

Violence Begins

Just two days after August 15, 1947, Independence Day, the boundary commission of Cyril Radcliffe announced the line of divide between India and Pakistan. This report was the last straw. My family learned about it at our Gurdwara, as the announcement swept through rural Punjabi villages. Now we knew that our village was definitely in Pakistan, though we thought it was a temporary situation. This was a worrisome and anxious moment for the men and women of my family.

During that year, in early August—before violence erupted in our area. I had just begun fifth grade, and I went to visit my aunt Piar Kaur, my father's sister. Her village was a few miles away, so I traveled alone on the train and was picked up by my uncle at the next railway station. After a two-week visit, I headed home. Violence in Punjab had increased markedly during that two-week period. For example, a train not far from our village was stopped by a gang of Muslims, and many Sikhs and Hindus onboard were slaughtered. I was very lucky not to have been on that train. This thought has come to my mind many times through the years.

Lord Mountbatten inspects a burned-out village in southwest Punjab, where 22 Sikhs and Hindus were killed and an estimated thousand homes destroyed during the lead-up to Partition.

Violence occurred on both sides of the line of demarcation, perpetrated by members of the three religions—Muslims, Hindus, and Sikhs.

In west Punjab, trains carrying villagers fleeing east were stopped and Hindus and Sikhs butchered by Muslims. Other trains were lit on fire. During the height of this mayhem, the religious identity of victims was ascertained by checking for circumcision (Muslim) and religious tattoos as well as a knowledge of religious scripture.

Our old life was gone, our connection to the land sundered.

Spirituality and God were somewhere in hiding. Religious fanaticism ruled. Old friendships disappeared. Muslims and Sikhs of the Chattha clan became enemies. (However, in many villages, a few loyal Muslims gave shelter to Hindus and Sikhs at the cost of their own lives.) Looters and hooligans had their day.

Sikhs were angry, and rightly so. They were aware of the cruelty against Sikh gurus and Sikhs individuals in the past by the Mughals. Now, through Partition, they had lost to Pakistan the fertile land of the canal colonies as well as their sacred shrines.

Once the Sikhs had ruled Punjab. Now they were homeless.

Angry Sikh refugees from North West Frontier, with the help of the local Sikh population and some help from the Sikh princely states, got organized into Sikh *jathas* (militias). They also got a helping hand from RSS (Rashtriya Swayamsevak Sangh), a militant Hindu organization.

These armed bands killed Muslims, burned houses, derailed trains, and killed Muslim refugees on their way to Pakistan. It was a game of tit for tat. (The Muslims of the state of Malerkotla, however, were not touched because of their sympathetic attitude toward the sons of the tenth guru as they were bricked in behind a wall, alive, at Sirhind, in the early 1700s by the ruling Mughals.) The fury of the *jathas* lasted for four to six weeks, and then calm returned.

Women suffered the worst violence. Many Sikh families killed their own wives, mothers, and daughters so they would not fall prey to Muslim men. Women were raped, forced to convert, and disfigured. Some Muslims promised safe exit to non-Muslim families if they handed over their young daughters, but in many cases the families were slaughtered anyway and the girls exploited. Women were the victims of their gender. This state of affairs was described by Shailendra, Amrita Pritam, and Shiv Kumar Batalvi in excellent poems.

Some classes of people mostly escaped this violence. Usually they were those whose positions afforded them better protection, including political leaders, the educated, the rich, army men, and civil servants. The middle class, farmers, and the poor suffered the most, even though they were the flag bearers of various freedom movements.

Sikh villagers in our area had three choices—flight, convert, or fight:

- **Leave everything behind and head for India.** This is what most people did. Farmers, whose livelihoods were tied up in their land, lost the most. Businessmen fared better because they had liquid assets and education, which they could take with them. A lot of money already had been exchanged between the banks of Pakistan and India as people of means transferred their resources.
- **Convert to Islam.** Some villagers—individuals as well as entire families—opted for conversion to avoid violence and migration.
- **Fight.** This was what the Sikhs in the village of Bhulair decided to do.

Shahidi Saka Bhulair (The Patriotic Story of Bhulair Chak No. 119)

This is the gruesome and tragic story of a battle for the soul of the village of Bhulair as narrated in a small booklet written in January 1948 by my distant uncle Dr. Virsa Singh Bajwa, who was

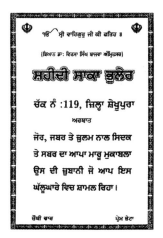

On left, cover of the booklet about the battle of Bhulair, written by (on right) Dr. Virsa Singh Bajwa.

born and raised in the village. Most of these events were corroborated by my elder brother Harbans Singh, who was a volunteer soldier in that battle.

BHULAIR CHAK NO. 119 was established by Virsa Singh Bajwa's ancestors, who had moved from another village, also called Bhulair, in the Tehsil Pasrur, Sialkot district, to take advantage of British land development. Bhulair Chak No. 119 was very close to Sangla Hill and to my village, Chak No. 46.

The villages in the Punjab canal colonies had been established mostly along religious lines. The residents of Bhulair were all Sikh farmers, though some support services were provided by *kamis* (laborers), who were mostly Muslim and Christian. Over time, these Sikh farmers became well-to-do, and their children were in various military and civil jobs. The villages surrounding Bhulair, meanwhile, were all Muslim. This fact made Bhulair more vulnerable to

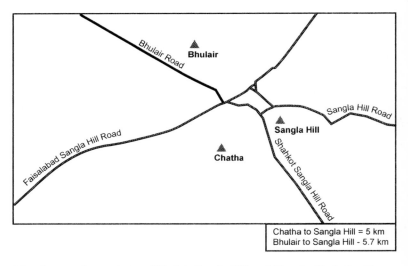

Chatha to Sangla Hill = 5 km
Bhulair to Sangla Hill - 5.7 km

Map showing the proximity of Bhulair, Sangla Hill, and Chattha Chak No. 46.

communal threat than other Sikh- and Hindu-majority areas, which were built on the other side of the Rakh Branch canal. The only way across the canal was by one of many bridges. Thus the village of Bhulair was in a particularly exposed location.

As the reality of a British exit from India and the partitioning of India dawned on people, the line of demarcation still was not certain. The boundary commission had started its work, but most of this was secret. Although India became free on August 15, 1947, the boundary commission report was delayed till August 17.

At some point during those unstable days of August, Bhulair and all the neighboring villages realized that they were now in *Pakistan*. Some villagers must have held out hope for peace. After all, Jinnah had assured non-Muslims that they would be treated fairly. His assurance and the lack of media made the situation muddier. Confusion persisted in the villages, and circumstances were changing fast.

Isolated events of violence against Sikhs increased. The leaders of Bhulair Chak No. 119 got worried and requested that all former residents living out of town come home to help. Some army soldiers answered the call and came home, with weapons. Virsa Singh Bajwa, an established forty-year-old doctor, left his medical job in Multan, as well. I was also told of a man named Arjan Singh, a soldier in the British army, who answered the call for help and deserted his regiment, arriving in Bhulair with a machine gun, prepared to fight for the protection of his village.

The animosity between Sikhs and Muslims got worse when some Muslim refugee families from Amritsar and Gurdaspur (both Hindu-dominant and Sikh-friendly) arrived in Muslim villages near Bhulair and gave exaggerated accounts of violence against Muslims in their previous towns.

The bad news got worse.

On August 25, a train from Sheikhupura to Sangla Hill was stopped on the way, and all Sikh and Hindu passengers were slaughtered. The bodies were thrown in a canal. (This was not the train massacre that occurred near the time I was traveling home from visiting my aunt but a different one.)

With all this happening, Bhulair got on a war footing. A meeting, led by village elders, was held in the Gurdwara, and all village families resolved their personal differences and pledged to fight for their safety.

Young men were advised to buy horses and weapons, legally or illegally; women were advised to wear a *kirpan* (dagger). Loyal Muslim blacksmiths made *kirpans* and spears. One young man started making bombs. One of these exploded, injuring one person. This resulted in police inquiry but no punishment. Carpenters and blacksmiths improvised guns from barrels of air pumps and batteries. Bullets were made in the village for guns. Roads to the village were cut off to prevent the entry of the police or the army. (The police force was all Muslim and was coordinating the attacks; it recruited informers, including one Sikh family. What was their payment? One Sikh informer was promised a gun license by the local magistrate for this betrayal, a small payment for his perfidy.) Word was spread for everyone to gather in the Gurdwara when they heard the siren of the *shankh* (conch shell).

The villagers were continually harassed by Muslims from neighboring villages wishing to intimidate and, perhaps, to scout the village. These *badmash* (bad characters) would occasionally show their presence, on horseback, in the vicinity of the village. And occasionally trucks full of hooligans would pass by. These were precursors of worse to come.

Local, well-meaning Muslims held a meeting in the village of Saranvali for peace and mutual safety, but it did nothing to stop the terrible momentum.

Sikhs from neighboring villages joined together to turn Bhulair into a garrison. Every Sikh family from a nearby village sent a young fighting volunteer. My family sent my eldest brother, S. Harbans Singh Chattha, who was about eighteen years old.

Rivalries within families disappeared, and everyone joined together in a single cause: to protect the village in case they were attacked. Sikhs are known for their courage in battle, and the fight for Bhulair was no different. The men were prepared to fight to the death.

The attack on the village of Bhulair occurred on August 31, 1947.

The initial attack was carried out by local bands of ill-organized militia. The Muslim attackers had not antici-

Harbans Singh Chattha, Amrik's older brother.

pated that villagers would be so organized, and many of the attackers were killed. Those attackers who survived then went to the local Muslim police commander and judge for help and were reinforced by members of the police and the army. They used automatic guns and rifles on the populace. The bullets came down like rain. Many villagers fought to the death, including the sharpshooter Arjan Singh, who fired till his ammunition ran out and he was killed. He was later honored in a poem describing his bravery: *Mare goli Arjana. Dege Dushman Darjana Wah Wah. Tere. Arjana.* (When Arjan fires, he kills enemies by the dozens, many cheers for great Arjan.)

On September 1, things got worse. Women, the disabled, and children of Bhulair were moved from house to house in an effort to keep them safe. Some found shelter in the homes of their loyal Muslim friends. But the shelter was only temporary.

As the police and the army moved into the village of Bhulair, women and young girls felt trapped. They began to think about death and suicide rather than attack or risk capture by the Muslim raiders. Some made the awful decision to kill themselves by throwing themselves into wells. Some asked to be shot to death by the men in their families rather than be taken captive. In my own family, Uncle Virsa Singh Bajwa shot his wife, my aunt Kartar Kaur, and their twelve-year-old daughter. Their bodies were thrown in the village well.

(Intentional honor killing has happened before in history. I recently visited the Masada fortress in Israel. This fortress was built atop a mountain by a Hasmonean king and further fortified by Herod the Great. Nearly a thousand Sicarii rebels and Jewish families were holed in there when Romans attacked them around 73–74 CE. The Jews of Masada chose to die at the hand of a fellow Jew rather than become Roman slaves.)

Despite all this, many Sikh women were captured alive. Some were later repatriated (found and reunited with their families in India). However, later, many women could not be traced and probably were converted to Islam and forced to marry Muslims.

According to calculations in Dr. Bajwa's booklet, about 350 Sikh men, women, and children of Bhulair were killed, missing, or abducted. About 1,000 Muslim attackers were killed.

By that evening, the police and the army had left. They probably ran short of ammunition or were afraid of reinforcements coming from other Sikh villages. Looters, however, stayed busy. They searched and ransacked homes, killing those who hid themselves. By the next day, September 2, the village was mostly empty. The village patriarch, Baba Amar Singh, refused to leave. He thought that his whole family had been killed and that life was no longer worth living. A loyal

Muslim persuaded him to leave and led him to a neighboring Sikh village; however, on the way, Baba Amar Singh was killed by a Muslim refugee from east Punjab. It was later learned that both his sons had survived.

The villagers of Bhulair sought refuge in neighboring Sikh villages across the canal where they had relatives. My uncle Virsa Singh and my brother Harbans Singh arrived in our village from Bhulair at 11 PM. Their clothes were bloodstained. I was awake to see and listen to them. They were depressed and spoke in low tones. Uncle had a bullet wound in his back that had exited through the groin.

After a few days, most of the villagers from Bhulair gathered at Nankana Sahib, site of a Sikh religious shrine. The injured were treated. With all this in view, even I as a little boy thought, *"azadi* is *barbadi."*

From Nankana Sahib, the injured were evacuated about fifty miles away via army vehicles to Amritsar, the largest town in eastern Punjab, which lies near the line of demarcation. Once they arrived, Master Tara Singh, head of the Akali Dal movement, took good care of them, and the refugees were allotted land at Batala, which had been owned by Muslims who had fled that town.

During this tragic time, many Muslim heroes helped Sikh families at the risk of their own lives. Some Muslim families of the village gave shelter and hid them, while others covered Sikh women with burqas and then took them to a Sikh camp.

Looking back seventy years later, I wonder if this slaughter could have been avoided. Our villages had many wise and educated leaders. Also, every Sikh village did not face this tragedy. I can now think and imagine why this tragedy occurred in Bhulair and not in all other villages in Punjab.

- Lack of communication. Newspapers had stopped publication. There was no telephone service. Villages had radios, but even the news was of little use because the situation was unclear and evolving.
- Geography. Bhulair Chak No. 119 was vulnerable because it was surrounded by many Muslim villages.
- Misleading assurances. Jinnah publically stated that minority groups would be treated well and that there would be no movement of population.
- Violence unexpected/underestimated. Many people wrongly believed that the violence would be temporary and that peace would prevail in time.
- Speed. Events moved too fast to comprehend.
- Timing. The boundary commission was slow to report.
- Experience of Bhulair. Other villages learned from Bhulair and decided to leave rather than stay and fight.
- British Army absent. Nobody at Delhi anticipated this violence and movement of population. The British Army could have been kept active for a few more months because the police force was mostly Muslim, with an anti-Sikh bias, who helped the attackers.
- Sikh leadership uncertain. The Sikh leadership was ignorant, locally and in New Delhi; hence the public was confused as events unfolded.

Could tragedy have been avoided? In hindsight, yes. However, irrational times = irrational thinking. A village cannot defeat a nation. The village of Bhulair—and the Sikhs who came to join the fight—stood no chance against the gathering forces of Muslims cleansing their new country of Sikhs and Hindus.

Part 3

Migration and Kaflas

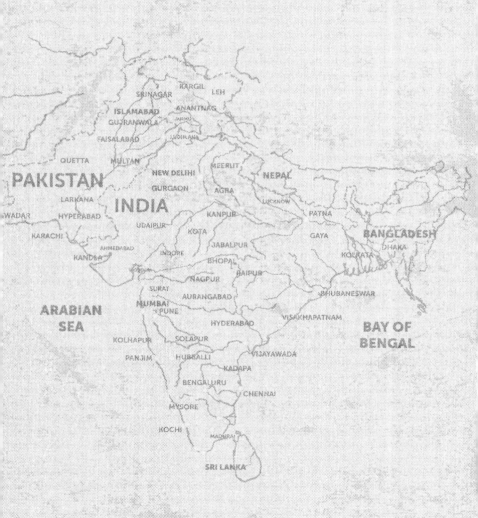

The Kafla *(Caravan) Begins*

The night my brother and a bloodied Virsa Singh arrived at our home in Chak No. 46, other Bhulair villagers also started arriving in our village. (Those with Sikh relatives in other villages went there.) It was clear to everybody in Chak No. 46 that there would be no protection for Sikhs in Pakistan in spite of assurances from Jinnah.

Fleeing villagers used many forms of transportation to evacuate their lands, including, for the lucky ones, overloaded trucks.

Refugees, many barefoot, drive bullock carts loaded with family possessions.

My grandfather was still hoping against hope that the violence was temporary; however, he soon changed his mind after discussion with the village elders and his sons.

The decision was made: our family would flee.

We quickly gathered a few clothes and jewelry. My grandfather had only Rs 135 with him, and that's all the money our family had for our journey.

Columns of Sikh and Hindu refugees from West Punjab approach Balloki Headworks as they move toward India.

Refugees en route.

My Journey

Day 1

We started our journey under cover of darkness on the night of September 1. We headed to the neighboring village of Burj, a trip of about two hours, to join a large *kafla* heading to India. As the caravan moved, more people from other villages joined us, and the caravan became longer. People were on foot, riding bullock carts, and on horseback. I was reminded of a trip my family had made the previous year to Nankana Sahib to celebrate the birthday of Guru Nanak, the founder of the Sikh faith. A similar caravan of bullock-drawn carts (*gaddas*) a mile long had headed to the holy city. The current caravan was no birthday celebration—not even for the birthday of two new nations.

The adults were in misery, terrified and unnerved. For them, the future was unknown. For them, *"azadi* is *barbadi."* They had every reason to think that way. But my cousins and I experienced no fear or anxiety.

Leaving our village was an especially big blow to my grandfather. He lost his land, home, prize-winning horses, and friends.

Heartbroken, he started his journey east, back to his roots in the original Chattha village in east Punjab where he had been born, sixty years after he left.

Day 2

The caravan continued through Burj and on to another small village. The inhabitants there were already prepared to join the caravan. The day before we arrived, the villagers had been busy cooking for us and making arrangements for our one-night stay. When the caravan stopped for the night, patriotism and kinship were felt by all; we were all Jat Sikh brethren and relatives. However, at this stage, any joy about Indian independence from the British was pushed back.

My grandfather made a last-ditch effort to assess the situation in Chattha Chak No. 46 and returned to our village on horseback, accompanied by my distant uncles Inder Singh and Arjan Singh. As the three men approached the village, they were rushed by a mob of men—their own kith and kin, Muslim Chatthas who had lived with them in the same village their whole lives. As the mob converged on them, wielding swords and knives, my grandfather turned his horse around and escaped, while Inder Singh and Arjan Singh ran into sugarcane fields to hide. The mob pursued them, and they were presumed to be killed. For many years, our family lived without knowing who had killed Inder Singh and Arjan Singh.

In the morning, the caravan pushed on.

Day 3

The next day, we reached the village of Loake. One of my distant uncle's in-laws lived in that village, so our family stayed at their home. Large-scale cooking—simple *dal* (lentils) and *roti* (bread)—was in progress to feed the refugees. We ate, but unfortunately, we could not take the food with us on the journey; there was no way to safely store food.

Many young men became drunk, and a few pistol shots were fired at the sky to challenge any enemies. It looked like a big wedding with an air of celebration—or a great denial of things to come. Maybe we Punjabis are raised to expect these adversities, a tendency that goes all the way back to our battle with Alexander the Great in 321 BCE.

Day 4

The caravan reached Jaranwala, the site of a big, sprawling encampment, one of the stopover locations on the way to India. (Jaranwala had been just a regular village till the migration began; then it turned into an encampment and place for caravans from various villages to amass.) An asphalt road connected this village to Lahore, the capital city of Punjab. At this camp, I saw the Sikh leader Giani Kartar Singh assuring people of a safe journey to India. He was a devout Sikh who maintained all symbols of Sikhism (*kesh* [uncut hair], *kirpan* [dagger], *kanga* [wooden comb], *kara* [steel bangle], and *kachha* [shorts]).

As we were preparing to look for a place to temporarily stay in this large camp, my father, S. Tara Singh, and my uncle, S. Shingara Singh, both army officers, suddenly drove up in an army vehicle with a driver and an Indian Army soldier with a gun. Our family was overjoyed! My father, whom I had not seen in seven or eight months, and my uncle had come to rescue us and transport us to India. The journey to the land of the free was in sight for us. They had been looking for us in all the neighboring camps, driving from place to place.

When the army vehicle appeared, many people rushed the truck to climb in, but the soldier in the truck kept them away. "Family first," declared my selfish father. (I don't fault him. Who wouldn't be selfish when your family's safety is at stake?) After our immediate family—my family plus all uncles and aunts and their children—were loaded onto the truck, there was room only for close relatives. In total, 135 relatives were able to get into the truck—but others could not be accommodated. They were forced to continue the slow, brutal migration with the caravan. One of our relatives left behind was a distant uncle named Akalia, who later in the journey lost his wife to cholera, leaving behind three little girls. For this tragedy, my father lived with guilt for the rest of his life.

The army vehicle headed to India, a trip of about eighty miles. The soldier stood on top of the truck with a gun to guard against any attack. The road had a continuous line of people on foot, in bullock carts, and on horseback. However, after a few miles, the road was empty. In our vehicle, we had easily outpaced the caravan. After that, we rarely saw anybody, because Sikhs from border villages had already migrated, leaving behind only Muslims, who remained in the villages.

Passing through Lahore, we found the once-bustling city abandoned and deserted. People stayed indoors because of a curfew—but also from fear. We reached the Indo-Pak border at Wagah just four hours after we left Jaranwala. We passed into India and continued on. When we reached Amritsar, we were greeted with *"bole so nihal!,"* a Sikh hurrah. Sikh committees had been set up to aid the arriving migrants. Roasted chickpeas were served as an afternoon snack, and an overnight stay was arranged at a *sarai* (guest house) at Harmandir Sahib (the famous Golden Temple). My father and uncle stayed at an army guest house.

In Amritsar, there were so many refugees that it looked to my ten-year-old eyes like all of humanity was in motion: people were moving with their few belongings, some on foot and some on bullock carts; others were rushing to railway stations; some were carrying their elder relatives on their backs. Everywhere there was misery and movement.

Day 5

The next day we headed to our ancestral village of Chattha—the village in the Gurdaspur district of India that my grandfather and his two brothers had left many years earlier when they struck out for the rich lands of west Punjab. In this village, we still had some land, but no house. Our land had been leased to some distant cousins whose families had not migrated to Chattha Chak No. 46 those many years ago. Though we left our ancestral village, we kept connected to our land. This small parcel, about twelve acres, owned by my grandfather and his two brothers, was our connection with our past—our *watan*, or homeland—and my family members would visit once a year to collect lease money. Now, with my family's arrival, these distant Chatthas felt threatened. They thought that if we decided to stay permanently, we might claim our leased land, so they wanted no part of us. They offered no hospitality and no refuge.

However, there were empty homes in that village, vacated by Muslims fleeing to Pakistan. We kids became like little looters, claiming anything we liked. I remember entering the empty house of a Muslim weaver. He had spun cloth in his *khadi* (weaving machine), and spools of thread were still lying around. We picked the spools up, thinking to use them for kite flying. Overall, there was nothing of value in those vacant homes. Either the former inhabitants had had enough time to pack, or maybe these homes had already been ransacked after the Muslims left. I assume the village adults also acquired some items left behind. Looting was prevalent all over Punjab, and one day my *mama* (mother cousin) Raghbir Singh Gill appeared with *thans* (bundle) of fabric, which he got by breaking into a freight train stationed at Firozpur railway station. He distributed his loot to all the relatives. (During this time looting and stealing for personal use was not considered a crime.)

We stayed in our native village for only a few days since the atmosphere in the village was less than hospitable. Our family started looking for another place. We were fortunate we had guns, which kept us safe. (Though the violence was now directed toward Muslims, not toward us, it was still prudent to keep guns for protection.)

Karnal

Even if my large family had chosen to settle back on our ancestral land, we knew a twelve-acre parcel could not sustain all of us, so we continued our journey to the easternmost part of Punjab, to a city called Karnal, now located in the state of Haryana, where land was more plentiful. By this point, it had been two weeks since we left Chak No. 46.

Although there was sufficient land in Karnal, it was of poor quality. Luckily, my folks had army connections and weapons, so we were able to easily grab land and properties in that period of chaos.

In Karnal, we first occupied a big, empty house that had once belonged to Liaquat Ali Khan, who later became prime minister of Pakistan. Later, because we needed more space for our extended family, we moved temporarily to empty army barracks, where we stayed for two weeks. After that, we moved into a home formerly belonging to a doctor in the city, which still had intact medical paraphernalia. A few weeks later, we moved yet again to a small town near Karnal where elite Muslim army officers had lived, and we stayed there for less than a week before moving again, this time to Gharaunda.

My family and I lived in the community center in Gharaunda for more than a year, and I attended fifth and sixth grades in the local middle school, finishing both years as the top student. It was morale boosting for me because back in Pakistan, I could not qualify for a fourth-grade merit scholarship examination at the district level. After doing well in fifth and sixth grades, I continued to be a top student in subsequent grades.

But even in school, we could not forget the turmoil we had experienced. Sometimes Hindu students made comments such as "*Hindu nu mil gia, hindustan, mussalmana nu Pakistan, te sikhan nu milia kacha kirpan.*" This translates to "Hindus got India, Muslims got Pakistan, and Sikhs only got shorts and sword." (The last two are symbols of Sikhism.) I heard this taunt frequently in my school.

Every morning, school assembly began with songs of praise and prayer in honor of Bapu Gandhi as well as Sardar Patel and Nehru. The national song "Vande Mataram" and the national anthem "Jana Gana Mana" became popular later. I was a member of the school choir.

One important event at this town stays in my memory whenever we talk about corruption. It pertained to temporary land allotment. This allotment was done by a local *tehsildar* (junior tax collector), who asked for a bribe before he would allot land to my family. My folks wanted to report this bribery to the local law enforcement agency, so they marked the bills they used to pay him. The bribery was brought to attention of a local police sub-inspector. Strangely, the sub-inspector—instead of taking action against the *tehsildar*—came to our residence and started beating my uncle with a bamboo stick, accusing him of illegally putting a signature on national currency. The *tehsildar* and the police officer were in cahoots on the bribery scam. I witnessed the whole scene, and it was my first encounter with bribery. It is sad that even in dire circumstances there are people willing to take advantage of others' helplessness.

Batala

My grandfather was upset by all this. He did not like this part of Punjab, because the culture and the language were different. We were now living in an area where people spoke mostly Hindi, and very little Punjabi. He made up his mind to go back to his roots in Gurdaspur district, and the family agreed. But instead of going back to our ancestral Chattha village, we landed in a small village called Bode di Khuhi, near Batala. There we sought shelter in a vacant mosque. Space was tight in the mosque, so my family made a small tent for my grandfather with a thatched bamboo roof, which leaked during the rains.

Along with my cousins, I enrolled at Khalsa High School in Batala (previously, it had been called Islamia High School). Later, I graduated from this school.

A few years later, the process of permanent rehabilitation and land allotment started under the auspices of the Rehabilitation Commission. My extended family was allotted land and a house in the village of Nawan Pind Mehmowala, near Batala. This became our permanent residence.

Over the years, many of us have left the village for education and better opportunity in big cities and other countries; very few of us live there today. This village, though, has remained my address on my Indian passport.

Hardial Singh Dhaliwal

This is the story of one of my relatives, Hardial. He was thirteen years old when he and his family were forced to leave their village and travel in a *kafla* to India.

Before Partition, Hardial had been living with his *mama* (maternal uncle) Gurdas Singh, a well-to-do farmer with approximately one hundred acres of good, irrigated land in the village of Chak No. 301, near the Jhang branch of a canal near Toba Tek Singh, in the district of Lyallpur (now called Faisalabad).

A few weeks before Partition, the local Sikh leaders Giani Kartar Singh and General Mohan Singh of the *Azad Hind Fauj* (Indian National Army) visited Chak No. 301 and told the farmers that they should not sell their harvest in a rush because there might not be a partition of Punjab. And if there was, people wouldn't be displaced. They further said that the non-Muslims living in Pakistan might have to pay taxes, and there might be no ban on cow slaughter (a big deal in those days). In the worst-case scenario, they suggested, all able-bodied Sikhs would be provided weapons and training for their protection.

Keeping their words in mind, the village was put on high alert and war footing. All able-bodied male adults and adolescents gathered in the village *rakkar* (community ground). At 6 AM the following morning, they were given training in using shotguns, spears, swords, and *gatka* (Sikh martial art).

Some violence against Hindus and Sikhs had already started in northwest India. Also, Bengal had experienced large-scale violence. In spite of Mahatma Gandhi's prayers for peace, violence continued. Local Sikh leaders, however, simply had no clarity regarding the situation.

Around August 14, Hardial's uncle sold his harvest. By this point, most people knew that Pakistan would be a reality and that Punjab would be divided into two. The actual boundaries had not been declared, but Hardial's uncle thought, "Why take a chance?" He was now fully convinced about Partition.

With a heavy heart, he and all the Sikh farmers in the village decided to flee with their families for India, leaving behind their workers, who were mostly Muslims. He was even more convinced when the body of a murdered relative was brought to him. A farmer from the relative's village had seen the dead body in a field and brought it to Hardial's uncle. The relative, who had lived in a neighboring village, had been killed on the 14th and his horse and gun taken by the assailants. Hardial and his uncle later learned the relative had been on his way to advise them to move to India.

The neighboring village, Nurpur, was all Muslim. Hardial's uncle had a *langotia yar* (close friend) named Nek Mohammed who lived there. Hardial's uncle asked Nek Mohammed to take care of the possessions he left behind, and Nek Mohammed agreed. Initially, his two sons came to pick up the possessions, but they ran back home to Nurpur for fear of getting killed. When Hardial's uncle reassured the boys that they would be safe, they returned and took his belongings.

Then, at midnight, under cover of darkness, Hardial and his family set out, bound for a neighboring Sikh village. For the journey, the family took four oxen to pull the cart, six water buffaloes, a horse, a goat, some clothes, and all their jewelry.

A few months earlier, Hardial had noticed a change in his Muslim classmates' behavior. For instance, they were less respectful to the Sikh boys and had started using derogatory words like "Sikhras." They would taunt Hardial and the other Sikh boys, saying that soon this would be a Muslim land and that Sikh boys would not be coming back to school after summer vacation.

Hardial's family reached Chak No. 298 on August 17. The villagers took good care of them, and they joined the *kafla* (caravan) that same day. Hardial was on horseback and in charge of the water buffaloes, which provided milk for their family. On the way, the water buffaloes got into a village *chapper* (pond) to quench their thirst and to cool down from the hot summer day. But the animals refused to come out, and he could not force them. On the advice of his uncle, Hardial abandoned them there to keep pace with the rest of caravan. Soon, the family's bullocks started to struggle. The carts were full and the weight was hard on the bullocks, so the family decided they had to lighten the load and threw many unnecessary objects off the carts. They did other things to lighten the load, too, including removing all the spun cotton in their quilts. Piles of *ruhn* (cotton) were all over the sides of the road, which indicated that many other families were taking the same action.

On August 18, after crossing the railroad, the caravan reached the fifth village of the journey. At this location, many feared that the caravan would be attacked because many Muslim villages were in this area. And indeed, a poorly organized gang attacked them. All the women, elderly, and children sought shelter in the local Sikh

Gurdwara, and the adult men were advised to get under the carts. Sikh horsemen with guns tried to protect the caravan, and the gang was repulsed. However, a few hours later, armed Muslims came back with police. (The only policemen left at this point were Muslims, and they supported gang activities.) Hardial and a young schoolteacher tried to hide from the attackers in a sugarcane field. When the gang began shooting, the teacher was hit by a bullet in the chest and died instantly. Hardial, close by, was saved. The raiders—trying to take young women and prized animals—could not come close to the caravan and ran away.

As soon as possible, the caravan left that village and moved on. As it went, the caravan became longer and longer as other Sikh families joined. Nobody in the caravan wanted to be in the rear, which was more vulnerable to attack, so the location of last few carts was decided by lottery.

The caravan circumvented the large encampment at Jaranwala (the camp my family and I reached on day 4 of our journey) and finally got on paved road that led to Lahore. (Thus far, the refugees had been traveling along dusty roads that ran beside the irrigation canal.)

On about day 6, the caravan came to a small roadside cement slab that read "Lahore 32 miles." After deliberating, caravan leaders decided that going to Lahore could be dangerous, so the caravan headed to the Balloki waterworks on the Ravi River. At that waterworks, the caravan would have had to cross a small bridge on an overflow water channel. The bridge was small and unstable, and only a few carts were allowed daily, which created a huge backlog of carts miles long. The road was narrow and slightly elevated.

At that point, the monsoon season started, turning fields on either side of the road into large swamps. Owing to the rising water level, the emergency overflow channel was opened. This sudden rush of water washed away the fragile bridge! Now there was nowhere to go. Everybody was stuck. Approximately five to seven thousand people in Hardial's caravan were trapped on this small, narrow road for almost six weeks. It was a nightmare. Although only a few fatalities were due to skirmishes, the waiting period was a death knell for many. Families ran out of food, and there was no sanitation, resulting in a cholera epidemic.

Day-to-day survival was a desperate enterprise.

Food, already meager, almost ran out when the caravan stalled. Initially, young men would go in the neighboring fields and collect whatever was edible, including unripe rice, which was plentiful in the swampy land. The unripe rice grain was thrashed and eaten. River water was boiled for drinking and cooking. Also, the bark of the acacia tree was used to make tea. Cooking was done on a *chulha*, and young men would collect the twigs of cotton plants to use for making the fire.

Everybody was out for himself. Hardial's uncle's father-in-law, also part of caravan, was discovered one day to have some sugar, which he had kept hidden. But he refused to give sugar even to his own grandchildren. It was sad when he died the next day. His body was disposed of in the river by attaching heavy stones to keep it underwater. As the days went by, many dead bodies that had been disposed of in this way came bobbing to the surface, bloated and stinking. The smell of dead bodies was everywhere.

Cleanliness and sanitation were impossible. To answer the call of nature, men would go a little way off in the fields. Women would go at dark behind bushes, with young men with guns at a distance providing security. Human waste was all over. Of course, nobody took a shower for weeks, and everybody smelled. Skin rashes due to malnutrition were common, as were scabies and lice. Malnutrition and poor hygiene brought on an epidemic of cholera. There were no physicians or paramedics or medical supplies. Hardial, however, remembers the sudden appearance of white nurses, most likely from the Red Cross or some other charity group, which tended to the caravan as best they could till the *kafla* reached the border.

Animals suffered alongside humans. For instance, there was no food for the oxen, so they lost drastic amounts of weight. Hardial's horse became skinny, and his goat had to be slaughtered.

After they had been stranded for some time, Hardial's family, who had some wheat, took the risk of taking it to a nearby Muslim village to have it ground into flour. Old Punjab had wheat- and flour-grinding mills called *kharas*. The Muslim owner of the mill wanted the outrageous payment of either two oxen or Rs 1,000 to provide this service. The family needed their bullocks to pull the cart for the journey, so they managed to collect Rs 1,000 from the caravan refugees. They shared the flour with the families that had helped them.

On October 3, news of the plight of this *kafla* came to the attention of authorities in India. The nurses had already arrived to help with medical needs, and now food began to be dropped by small-propeller planes. The pilot had to be precise with the drops because if the packets didn't land on the road, they'd land in the water on the sides of the road, and the food would be ruined. The spoiled packets were used for animal fodder.

Everybody was for himself, more than ever. There was no pity for anybody. As food packets were dropped, people ran and fought for food like dogs. Some people did not realize the size and weight of the packets coming down from the sky, and they ended up with serious head and neck injuries.

Since this human disaster affected both nations, Pakistan and

India, the governments agreed to provide the caravans with Pakistani and Indian army protection.

The bridge on the overflow channel was finally reconstructed by the Pakistan corps of engineers after a wait of five or six weeks.

After the bridge was rebuilt, four hundred to five hundred carts passed along to the other side. Hardial's family continue to wait. More dead bodies were seen. Nurses continued giving pills and injections. Finally, Hardial's family's turn to cross came seven days after the bridge was rebuilt.

After the caravan crossed the river, two armed soldiers in a jeep (part of a Gorkha regiment) escorted it to a camp established by the government of Punjab.

There, each family was provided a tent and a ration of rice and *dal* for three days. (Each person was fingerprinted, so he or she got only one share.) Families were also given three days to determine their route: would they go to Amritsar or to Kasur? After three days, these families would have to move on, and more families who had recently crossed the bridge would take their place. Army protection prevented any further attacks on the *kafla*.

Hardial's family opted to travel toward Kasur and continue on toward India. The road sign read "Patti 16 miles"—the distance to an Indian border town. The caravan continued through the village of Bhai Feruman. It crossed the border into India near the town of Valtoha, in the Amritsar district. As the caravan entered India, it was greeted by a jubilant crowd that provided the refugees with food. By this time, the boundary commission had defined the Indo-Pak border.

As people found relatives in Punjab to take them in, the size of the caravan began to shrink.

Hardial and his family continued with the caravan to the town of Beas, and along the way they crossed a small river named Baei. The water level was high, and the river difficult to cross, but they were able to find a shallow part and cross.

By the time of the big festival of Diwali—almost two and a half months after the night they left their village—Hardial and his family finally reached Ludhiana. The caravan had by this time dwindled, and they parked their cart in the Rakh Bagh area of Ludhiana. Hardial's uncle was politically well connected and soon was temporarily allotted five acres of land and a house in the village of Nurpur (not to be confused with the village of "Nurpur" near where Hardial was originally from). Nurpur was situated between the Satluj River and Buddha Nala (a seasonal river). The village was swampy and produced many mosquitoes. It was not worthy of permanent residence. This village's Muslim population had left, and plenty of acreage was planted with *Arbi* (taro), a type of vegetable. Every day, Hardial would haul arbi to the market at Ludhiana.

Finally, the family was permanently allotted land and a house at Raikot, in the district of Ludhiana. There were many big homes in town, and Hardial's family settled in a reasonably good accommodation.

With the family finally in a permanent home, Hardial resumed his schooling. He attended seventh and eighth grades at Patiala Khalsa High School and stayed with close relatives. He did ninth and tenth grades at Gurusar Sidhar, living in a hostel near Raikot and paying Rs 40 per month for boarding and lodging. He was a hostel prefect (student administrator). After high school, he attended Khalsa College at Amritsar and lived with a family a few miles from the college. That family had been a minor royalty in the past and owned a *sarai* (inn) as well as a *bunga* (rest house) in the vicinity of Harmandir Sahib (the Golden Temple). He occasionally stayed at the inn as well. However, he was unhappy and returned to school at Gurusar Sidhar, which had been upgraded to a college. He was a bright student.

Despite the ordeal of the caravan and the upheaval of resettling, Hardial earned a BA in math and subsequently a BT, or bachelor in teaching, and started teaching at B. N. Khalsa High School. He did extensive teaching and tutoring, and his students' grades improved. Very soon he was promoted to headmaster. He, however, did not like to be called Master Ji (teacher) when he was with well-placed family members whose professions were of higher status than that of teacher. He decided to venture overseas and was admitted to the Royal Technical College in the UK. Before going to England, he married Surjit, also a schoolteacher. While in England, money was scarce and a new baby arrived; he found he could not finish his studies, so he took a job after two and a half years of study. He later earned a degree in engineering at Westland Aircraft Co. for aeronautical maintenance.

In 1968, he moved to Canada and worked at Bombardier as a pre-flight inspector and navigation engineer. He left that job and taught math and technical vocational drafting from 1973 to 2000. After retirement, he and Surjit moved to Ottawa, where he has worked for over thirteen years at Walmart. He welcomes and provides help to elderly shoppers. He has a daughter, an MD and JD, who works for WHO (World Health Organization)) and a son who is an electrician. Hardial had a long journey and successful destination. But the memory of Partition still haunts him.

Ajit Singh Chattha

A jit is a longtime friend of mine who also had to flee with his family from their village in west Punjab when he was a child.

Ajit Singh Chattha (not to be confused with my older brother Ajit Singh Chattha) was ten years old when he and his family were forced to migrate to India. They belonged to the Chattha clan but, like my family, had over time separated geographically from other Chatthas. He grew up in Chak No. 349, in the district of Montgomery (subdistrict Pakpattan). Unfortunately, he lost his father when he was only six years old.

Like many other newly created villages, the population of Chak No. 349 was segregated along religious lines. In the village were landowners—both Sikh and Muslim—and support providers such as sharecroppers, carpenters, blacksmiths, and water carriers. These jobs, called *kami* (labor class), were done by both Muslims and Sikhs. The shopkeeper was usually a Sikh or Hindu. There were some Christian villagers, and the villagers called them "Isaiahs."

When Partition happened, the news spread to his village by word of mouth—there was no newspaper, radio, or TV—that Pakistan had been created and that Sikhs and Hindus had to leave the country. Ajit Singh and his mother, along with other family members, left early the next morning, August 15, at the crowing of the rooster, and headed to the city of Arifwala.

Approximately ten thousand Sikh families gathered there. These families carried their belongings on bullock carts loaded to the top. A big camp was organized at a large, open area, and his uncle S. Hazara Singh Gill was placed in charge of the camp. He was a well-to-do farmer, and the British had designated him *zaildar* (county executive). On August 16, the caravan started its journey to east Punjab.

Gradually, others joined the caravan, and it became approximately ten miles long. People were on foot and on horses. The old, infirm, and children were carried on *gaddas* (carts). Many horse riders carried guns, licensed by the British. These men provided security, helped the caravan to move, and helped fix disabled carts. The caravan moved slowly, covering only six or seven miles per day. At dusk, the caravan would stop and create a temporary camp. The gunmen provide security to the camp at night on a rotating basis. The next day, the journey would begin again on a narrow road on the bank of an irrigation canal.

It took ten days to cover approximately sixty miles to Balloki Headworks, a dam on the Ravi River. India was on the other side of this headworks.

Ajit's family's food consisted of *dal* and *roti*. The people of the caravan collected rainwater in large utensils for drinking and cooking. Women relieved themselves in darkness behind bushes as men stood guard at a distance. Nobody showered for days, and everyone smelled. Animals were fed *shatala* (a green fodder grown only to feed animals). Ajit passed by many bloated dead bodies on the roadside left from the earlier part of the caravan. The foul smell was inescapable. The caravan Ajit Singh traveled in did not experience enemy attacks or cholera; however, people suffered from malnutrition and skin rashes. After reaching India, Ajit's family was allotted temporary land and a house, but they decided to live temporarily with the sister of Uncle Hazara Singh Gill in the village of Sarhali, in Amritsar district. The family took this journey by passenger train, which was overcrowded, so they bought a ladder for Rs 10 and got on the roof of the train, where they contended with very hot, overcrowded, dangerous conditions. Ajit Singh saw a few people fall from the roof of the moving train.

The train traveled more than eighty miles, from Ferozepur to Jalandhar and ending at Amritsar. When the family arrived in Amritsar, they rode a bus to the village of Sirhali, twenty miles away.

During their migration, Ajit Singh's family was sometimes without food for one or two days. This mostly happened in India as the caravan gradually shrunk as people went to their respective destinations in India and the charities that had supported the refugees began pulling out. In the village of Sirhali, Uncle Hazara Singh's brother-in-law was an influential retired Subedar-major (above a noncommissioned officer) from the British Army. He helped Ajit Singh's family find temporary land and a house, where they stayed for approximately four months.

The rehabilitation commission finally allotted them permanent land and a house at the village of Bharowal, near the city of Tarn Taran, in Amritsar district, but they had much less land than they did in Pakistan.

After settling in India, Ajit Singh pursued his studies. He had completed fifth grade in his village in Pakistan. It had been a one-teacher school run by a *maulvi* (Muslim religious preacher). He went to a school at Fatehabad, in India, and completed sixth, seventh, and eighth grades. He completed ninth grade at Guru Angad Khalsa High School in Khadoor Sahib, Punjab, and tenth grade at Guru Gobind Singh High School.

He finished his BSc at DAV college, Jalandhar, Punjab. He spent one year in law college in the same city, and then headed to the United States, where he attended Cal Poly Technical Institute, San Luis Obispo College; Sacramento State College; and San Jose State College. To support himself, he worked on a Sikh farm in Yuba City. He was smart and was able to get a job without a proper visa. He later joined Raytheon, where he was promoted to manager. He subsequently joined National Semiconductor as senior director of quality control, retiring after twenty-five years. He and his wife, Sawaranjit, have two sons. He is one of the earliest Sikhs to work in the corporate world in the Bay Area and is among the Who's Who in Northern California. He considers himself very fortunate to be raised by his single mother and many members of his extended family. His journey was not a smooth road. He paved his way with hard work and willpower.

When I asked him about the partition of Punjab, Ajit Singh became emotional and wondered why people with the same cultural background could not live together at that time, though they had lived together peacefully for many centuries. He wished for a united Punjab and that we could have avoided the tragedy of Partition.

Mohinder

I have added a brief description of the ordeal my cousin sister, Mohinder, and her family went through during their journey in a caravan to India. Mohinder is the daughter of my mother's younger sister. Because of her young age at the time of Partition—she was five years old—she recalls only important events, most of them tragic.

Before Partition, Mohinder's family lived in Chak No. 294, part of the canal colonies. Her father, Man Singh Parwana, was a poet, a communist activist, and a high school graduate. ("Parwana"—a small insect that hoovers around a flame and ultimately gets burned— was a pseudonym.) Like the Sikhs of the village of Bhulair, they also belonged to the Bajwa clan, which was originally from Sialkot and is now a part of Pakistan. Because of his education, Mohinder's father was aware of the coming Partition.

The violence sweeping across India was felt in Chak No. 294. Two events prompted the exodus of Mohinder's family: a neighboring Sikh village was attacked, and the villagers learned what had happened at Bhulair. The writing was on the wall. For their safety, they felt they must leave.

Mohinder's family loaded their belongings on a *gadda* (cart), placed Grandfather Pashaura Singh on a horse, and began their journey around the last week of August. She remembers reaching the Jaranwala refugee camp—the camp my own family reached on day 4 of our journey. After one night's stay, my brother Harbans found her family. When my father and uncle arrived in the camp with the army vehicle, Mohinder and her family ran toward the army truck, already packed with other members of our family, hoping to wedge in. However, there was just no room. In spite of their pleadings, we could not fit them in; the vehicle was already overloaded. In the tumult, Mohinder's six-month-old brother, Iqbal, became semiconscious from exhaustion and hunger.

Mohinder's distraught family—including baby Iqbal—had no choice but to continue on with the caravan. (It was the same caravan in which Hardial Dhaliwal traveled.)

The caravan was stuck for six weeks at the Balloki Headworks. This was the most difficult time for the family, who struggled with a lack of day-to-day needs. For instance, they had no shelter and no clean water, and they lacked sufficient food.

Then more tragedy: Mohinder's mother, Bhagwant Kaur, developed cholera—which was sweeping through the travelers—and became unconscious. Luckily, she survived. Two days later, Mohinder's aunt—mother to four small daughters—fell sick. The aunt begged her brothers and father to save her. Had there been medical care, perhaps she would've recovered. But the refugees had nowhere to turn; there was no aid, no assistance. It was a desperate time. Before long, a young life was gone. The aunt's body was wrapped in a *khes* (cotton blanket), secured with rope wrapped round the blanket, anchored with a heavy stone, and placed in the water of the headworks.

Many people died each day and were given this unceremonial send-off. With the masses stranded at the headworks, the already acute shortage of food grew even worse. Lentils were the staple, but people ran short. They resorted to using the bark of the acacia for tea; however, soon even all the bark was gone. Finally, after approximately two months, the family reached India, but the family's sorrow continued: the baby of Mohinder's aunt also died.

Once in India, Mohinder's family stayed for a short time in Rasool Pur in east Punjab to rest and regroup. Once there, Mohinder's mother, for a short time, made a living by sewing clothes for others. Eventually, the family received a permanent land allotment at Behbal Chak in the Gurdaspur district.

During the long journey, the family had been accompanied by two very loyal Muslim or Christian employees, who came along to help. These two individuals stayed in Behbal Chak for six months, helping the family with day-to-day chores, till the family was resettled. My uncle, Mohinder's father, helped these two loyal individuals cross the border back into Pakistan at the village of Wagah.

Of all the family belongings, the items the family brought with them were a *parat* (a large, flat brass dish used for kneading flour, usually used during weddings) as well as a *gaggar* (a large brass container to store water). These had been part of the dowry of Mohinder's mother. The *parat* and the *gaggar* were passed down to Mohinder, and she treasures them. Every year she ceremonially polishes them. (Mohinder married my cousin Daljit Singh Chattha, who retired as a senior executive in Punjab judiciary.)

When I asked Mohinder about her most emotional memory of Partition, she said she cannot forget the cries of her dying aunt and how she begged for medical help, which was not available. Mohinder also remembers the days of poverty after her family reached safety, when her mom worked as seamstress to put food on the table. Everything else is forgotten now.

Animals and the Caravan

During natural and human calamities, animals suffer as much as humans, according to author Hilda Kean. During World War II, for instance, approximately 400,000 cats and dogs were euthanized in London alone because they could not be cared for. The partition of Punjab was no exception. Animals died of malnutrition and exhaustion and suffered the emotional trauma of losing their loving masters.

Punjabi farmers loved their animals. Land and animals were often their only assets, and cows and buffaloes were frequently gifted as dowry.

When we lived in Chattha Chak No. 46, my family owned many buffaloes, cows, and bullocks. We also owned two horses and a few goats. The goats were raised to be slaughtered on family occasions, usually a marriage. (Over time, the bullocks were replaced with tractors and the horses with motorcycle and cars.)

From the time he was a young boy, my uncle Balkar Singh Chattha, my father's youngest brother, refused to go to school. Instead, he took charge of the family animal stock. He loved our domestic animals and gave them names. His favorite young water buffalo was a *bhuri chotti* (a blond and brown young buffalo).

My uncle took loving care of his herd, including oiling their horns to look shiny. He would also place decorative jingle bells in the animals' manes, which made a melodious sound as the herd headed home after grazing. In addition, he owned a pet dog and a batera (a quail), which he used for fighting, similar to cockfighting. (The batera and the partridge are part of elite Punjabi cuisine.) Uncle would domesticate the bird in his leisure hours by holding it in his hand and feeding it small pieces of almond and butter to make it stronger for the fight. Uncle also was a good wrestler and had the nickname "Palwan Kikkar Singh," after the name of a local wrestler. I would carry his wrestling paraphernalia, which consisted of underwears called *Jhanghera* and *Sutna* and a small bottle of oil. I was his assistant till I reached college. (His wrestling career was cut short by a surgical operation for a cyst in his belly.)

Because we fled from our village in a hurry, our animals were all left behind except the bullocks, a horse, and a dog. Uncle Balkar Singh was hoping against hope that he would be able to go back to take care of the rest. However, the experience of a distant family member changed his mind: my distant uncle Arjan Singh tried to return to our village to look after his animals the day after we fled. However, once there, he was chased by a mob of Muslims. He tried to hide in a sugarcane field but was found and killed. This was enough for Uncle Balkar Singh to think, "All is lost." All his livestock was most likely looted.

Once our family was able to board the army truck at the Jaranwala camp, we gave our bullocks to others. Perhaps the bullocks helped another family survive. Who knows?

Balkar Singh's poor dog tried to get in the army truck but could not. He followed the truck for a while, and my uncle deliberately turned his head so as not to look at him.

Once in India, my uncle kept his deep love for animals. He bought a bull from the animal husbandry department and charged Rs 2 for his bull's service as a sire. On many occasions, the bull was overworked and had no interest in pursuing his duty. Uncle Balkar Singh's customers, often farmers from a neighboring village, would be kept waiting and irritated. Uncle had learned various maneuvers over the years to encourage the bull; so sooner or later, the job would get done, and Uncle would get his two rupees.

On many occasions, I assisted him in catching a batera for his hobby of bird fighting. We would stretch a long rope net across a wheat field and walk forward, cornering the little bird in the net. These were the village hobbies of days gone by.

Stories of Partition rarely mention the plight of animals that were part of families in the caravan. But animals often suffered alongside humans. Animals that accompanied the caravan often included the following:

o Bullocks or oxen. These pulled the carts. Without them, nothing could move.
o Horses. For a well-to-do Jat Sikh farmer, his horse was a symbol of prestige. A Jat Sikh farmer on horseback, with a gun on his shoulder and a dog at the heel, was the subject of envy in the village. At that time, horses were the only mode of transport.
o Water buffaloes. These meant wealth for a farmer; however, they didn't last long with the caravan.
o Goats. Some villagers brought their goats when they fled.
o Family dogs. Pet dogs accompanied some villagers when they fled, but they became fatigued, starved, and suffered from a lack of attention. Other pets, such as birds, were not popular in Punjabi society.

When Hardial Singh Dhaliwal's family joined the caravan, they took with them six bullocks (to pull the cart in rotation), water buffaloes (which they lost when the animals refused to leave the pond), a horse, and a goat. The goat was an alternate source of milk to the buffaloes. (Goats had developed respect from the populace because of Mahatma Gandhi, who advocated that goat milk was good for the brain.) The goat continued the journey until the family reached the Balloki Headworks. There, heavy rains caused flooding in the fields on the sides of the road, so there was little grazing or fodder, previous animals having stripped all the leaves from the trees. With little to eat, the goat grew emaciated and unable to produce milk. When the caravan was stalled for several weeks, the family ran short of food, and the goat was sacrificed and used to feed the family.

The family horse also suffered from lack of grazing and fodder and became starved, her ribcage prominent against her emaciated frame. However, when Hardial rode her, she did not rebel. One day, she was tied to a tree trunk with a rope and became restless. She wanted to eat, drink, and be free. Suddenly, she reared and yanked the rope, which broke, causing her to fall over backward and quickly die. Hardial was sad and guilt-ridden. He had loved that horse and would miss her companionship. She was buried in a shallow grave, like the grave of an unknown soldier who died for freedom. Unlike the water buffaloes, she had reached free India by the time of her death. The bullocks—having rested when the caravan was held up at the Balloki Headworks—fulfilled their duty, pulling Hardial's family to India.

In general, dogs moved along unleashed with the caravan and found their own food and water. Unlike in the West, dogs in India are not afforded love and respect. The caravan did not have any roosters or hens, which would have been more trouble than they were worth.

After we settled in our final home in India, my grandfather bought and rode a horse. We later put the horse to use pulling water at a Persian well because we did not have bullocks or water buffaloes. She was not prepared for this duty. She got angry, revolted, threw the rider, and made grunting noises of displeasure; but she carried out her duties till she died of old age. She was put to rest in a deep grave near the peepal tree a little distance from my grandfather's bed. For many years, I could locate her grave.

It is contrary to human dignity to cause animals to suffer or die needlessly.
—Catechism of the Catholic Church (2418)

Part 4

Post-Partition Years

Life in a Refugee Camp

When Sikhs arrived in India from Pakistan, but before permanent homes could be allotted to them, most lived in refugee camps. Most of the information in this section was provided by my late eldest brother, S. Harbans Singh Chattha. He was a student in Khalsa College Lyallpur (now called Faisalabad, in Pakistan). He did not finish his degree, but later Punjab University awarded him a degree based on his volunteer work in refugee camps.

In the years immediately following 1947, the population was very patriotic and widely involved in charity organizations that aided refugees before they moved to their allotted permanent land and homes in east Punjab. They did their best to relieve the suffering of their fellow Punjabis. Almost every big city in east Punjab had camps, whether big or small. The city of Patiala had two: a big camp for arriving Sikhs and Hindus, set up in a stadium, and a smaller camp for displaced Muslims waiting to depart for Pakistan at Fort Bahadurgarh. Both camps had been set up by the Maharaja of Patiala.

Life in the camps was bearable, especially after the suffering and turmoil of the migration. People began to try to find a sense of normality,

Hindu evacuees at the Punjab Scouts Camp, Lyallpur. An estimated fifty thousand evacuees were crowded together in buildings and improvised tents.

even though they were living in abnormal conditions. Some marriage proposals and marriages even took place in the camps. My own maternal uncle had a quick wedding in the camp, only to find out later that the girl was mentally challenged. This marriage lasted only three or four weeks. He later got remarried and raised a successful family.

Poor hygienic conditions caused an epidemic of scabies and lice, probably left over from the traveling caravans. DDT, not banned at the time, was used extensively on refugees' scalps. Luckily, no outbreaks of cholera, smallpox, or polio occurred. In the camps, food was adequate, with *dal* and *roti* as staples.

But people were very angry and traumatized over losing their loved ones and all their belongings. I was told that once, when Nehru was visiting a refugee camp, a man slapped him and said, "Give my mother back to me! Bring my sisters to me!" (Khan).

Most of the refugee camps were later folded, but some continued permanently as shantytowns. Even today there is one near Batala, occupied by people called *mahashas*. This colony has improved, with many permanent brick homes, water, and electricity. The refugees from west Punjab in this shantytown were generally not farmers but mostly helpers in various trades. Most of them came from the Jhang and Multan districts of west Punjab. Many got privileges similar to affirmative action programs in the United States and got good jobs. The well-to-do and well-connected left the camps and became part of the mainstream Punjabi community.

Repatriation

In the chaos of the migration, villagers were inadvertently, and sometimes intentionally, left behind as their family fled across the line of demarcation. Many times, the people left behind were women.

Some families stayed behind, thinking it would be a temporary situation; others were disabled and elderly and could not easily migrate. Some had a fear of settling in a new country. Some were simply accidentally left behind in the chaos of abandoning a village. Many women were captured and kept by raiders—taken from villages, from *kaflas*, from trains. No place offered complete safety, especially for a woman traveling without a family to offer protection. It was a religious war, and rape was a frequent weapon.

Captured women—forced to stay in Pakistan and to convert—found themselves trapped in a hostile religious environment with oftentimes hostile captors. With forced marriage, and accompanying pregnancy and motherhood, these women found themselves in a complicated situation. They were victims, yet many faced further victimization if they returned to their families in east Punjab because of cultural and religious thinking that blamed and marginalized women who had been raped, forcibly married, or forcibly converted to Islam. (Adding to the complexity, Sikh and Hindu women who gave birth from forced marriages to Muslim men had, according to law, to leave their infants behind in Pakistan when they were sent east to reunite with their families.)

After Partition, as both India and Pakistan began to deal with the aftermath of the great migration, one of the pressing issues for the newly arrived migrants was reclaiming their women (and men) left behind or abducted.

Both countries decided to restore the abducted to their families, who had now relocated to a different country. In September 1947, Nehru and Liaquat Ali Khan together toured districts in Punjab and vowed to reunite families that had been violently split apart through abduction. The Abducted Persons (Recovery and Restoration) Act was passed in 1949. Relatives from India went to Pakistan to get their loved ones; and people from Pakistan came to India for the same reason. The abducted women were usually thankful to be rescued and reunited with their families. But it wasn't always as simple as that. Some women had, during the many months since their abduction, reconciled themselves to their new life. Perhaps they were better treated by the new husband than they had been by their birth family or former husband. Perhaps they had more economic stability and resources with the new husband. Perhaps they had given birth and wanted to stay with the child. Perhaps they even grew to accept and love the new husband. But now, the government intervened, forcing them to leave. As women, they had almost no say. They were usually located and conveyed across the border.

I knew of a few women who were recovered.

One was a young Muslim woman kept for a time by my distant uncle. She had been a member of a *kafla* traveling west, heading to

Pakistan. This caravan had been attacked and looted by a Sikh *jatha* (militia). In addition to robbing the Muslim refugees of their belongings, members of the militia abducted this young girl, who was subsequently was rescued from the *jatha* by my distant uncle, who was single. What subsequently happened to her is most tragic and shameful for our family. This man kept the Muslim girl as a wife. The Sikhs who gave us shelter in Karnal (where we arrived two weeks after fleeing Chak No. 46) did not like this, so we were forced to leave. We then moved to a small town called Gharaunda, not far from Karnal. We lived in a *panchayat ghar* (community center), and my distant uncle moved into a nearby house with the girl.

The entire time she was kept by my uncle, I never saw her. I glimpsed her only when she finally left for Pakistan, as part of an exchange of people reuniting with their families.

On that day, an army officer of Pakistan appeared at our new house in a vehicle with two armed soldiers. It was the girl's brother, come to take his sister to Pakistan to join her family. There was rumor that she was pregnant by then, which upset her brother, but he agreed to take her to Pakistan anyway. As she left, she thanked our family for saving her life and protecting her from violent Sikhs and Hindus. My distant uncle was unhappy to lose his wife.

Though I don't know what the adults in my family thought of this situation since they never discussed sensitive matters with us children, as I reflect on this seventy years later, I can only conclude that even kind, civilized people lose their senses in a situation as stressful as Partition was.

The story of this girl haunts me anytime I think about Partition. What happened to her once she reached Pakistan? Was she killed by her family because she'd had a relationship with a non-Muslim? Honor killing was common practice in many Muslim tribes at that time. Did she have a baby from a Sikh father? I have no knowledge. Maybe she had her own story to tell. I seek her apology, and God bless her wherever she may be.

Another story I heard happened during the attack on the village of Bhulair. Many women were abducted or forcibly taken by Muslims. The Sikh wife of one of our distant relatives was captured, and she was married to a local Muslim. Her family, including her Sikh husband, now in east Punjab, learned her whereabouts and went to Pakistan to get her, about three years after he last saw her. When her Sikh husband, with the help of members of the Indian Army, reached the village where she was living, they found her reading the Quran. She had converted to Islam and refused to go to India; she said she was reconciled to her fate.

Another example of forced conversion happened in my village, Chak No. 46. During my childhood, I frequently saw one elderly man with his two grandchildren, who lived in a nearby village. These children had lost their parents, so their elderly grandfather was their caretaker. During the upheaval of 1947, he felt unable to endure the hardships of migration at his age, so he chose to remain in his village with the children. After Partition, in desperation, he and the children converted to Islam so they could continue to live in their home. The grandson grew up and was married to a Muslim girl from our own village. There is also the remarkable story of Boota Singh, an ex-serviceman from a village near Jalandhar, India. He fought during World War II at the Burmese front under the command of Mountbatten. He was middle-aged and single and very keen to get married. During communal riots, he saved a Muslim girl named Zainab. He later fell in love and married her. They had two daughters. As ill luck would have it, authorities snatched his wife ten to twelve years later and repatriated her to Pakistan. Boota Singh ventured to Pakistan with one of his daughters to get his beloved wife back. While in Pakistan he even converted to Islam. His wife, under pressure from her parents, refused to recognize him as her husband. Boota Singh, desperate, committed suicide by jumping in front of a train at Shahdara, near Lahore. The people of Lahore thronged to the hospital where his body lay. He was given a lover's ceremonial funeral and put to rest at Miani Sahib graveyard.

Zainab Boota's love story was one-sided. Even though Zainab suffered through communal riots, she did not stand up to her parents and society to glorify her love for Boota Singh, father of her two daughters. Her family did not even allow his burial in the village. You can look at her situation in two ways: did she betray her husband, or was she compelled to conform to the norms of her society?

Recently, an elderly Sikh women living in Bombay approached a visiting Punjabi singer from Pakistan and asked for his help to meet her two Muslim sons living in Pakistan. The kind-hearted singer was successful in fulfilling her last wish. Repatriation eventually involved even people in jails and mental asylums. In the short story "Toba Tek Singh," written in 1953, author Saadat Hasan Manto describes the fate of the fictional Bishan Singh, a Sikh living in a Pakistani insane asylum and forced, a few years after Partition in an inmate swap between Pakistan and India, to go to India. But Bishan Singh had land in the district of Toba Tek Singh, and no one—not guards, not visitors—could tell the insane man in what country Toba Tek Singh now lay. He became obsessed, asking whether his land was in Pakistan or Hindustan. When he was transported to Wagah, the Indo-Pak border crossing, he lay down between the two countries—barbed wire separating him from Pakistan on one side, and barbed wire separating him from India on the other—on a piece of land that had no name. Manto had other wrenching stories from the mental asylum. Who is insane? Maybe it was the dividers of Punjab.

These tragic stories of Partition have no end. There are ghastly stories of abducted and abused women on both sides of divided Punjab during this unfortunate time in our history. Amrita Pritam, a Punjabi poet laureate, in her famous poem, wrote, *"Ajj aakhan* Waris *Shah nu kiton kabran vichon bol"* (I want the poet Waris Shah to speak from his grave and address the plight of the daughters of Punjab).

Repatriation on religious grounds is unique to India, especially Punjab. Although the idea of repatriation seems straightforward and good as policy, it was, in practice, difficult, because humans and human relationships are complicated.

Rehabilitation (Resettlement)

The massive numbers of Hindus and Sikhs newly displaced from Pakistan had to be resettled in India. This resettlement process, called rehabilitation, was a monumental task, and the government set up a commission for this purpose called the East Punjab Refugees Rehabilitation (Registration of Land Claims) Act in 1948.

S. Tarlok Singh, of the Indian Civil Service, was the first general director of rural rehabilitation. The ICS officers of those days had dignity, power, and honesty; there was much less corruption than there is today. (The ICS cadre was changed to the Indian Administration Service [IAS] after Independence. The current IAS cadre is politicized and became impotent because authority was shifted to elected leaders, where corruption begins.)

S. Tarlok Singh would eventually oversee the largest land resettlement operation in the world to date, headquartered at Jalandhar, in east Punjab. He was a man with great integrity who worked hard. My father told me that Tarlok Singh had more gray hair in his beard on one side than the other, which was attributed to his constant exposure to light from a table lamp during his long hours of work.

The land and property that Muslims left behind in east Punjab was less valuable than what Hindus and Sikhs left behind in west Punjab; hence migrants to east Punjab had a lesser pie to share. (The refugee villagers called this reduction a "Tarloki cut," after the name of the commissioner.) The Rehabilitation Commission also got requests that families and neighbors be settled together, much as they had been in west Punjab. Sometimes an entire village requested to be relocated all together.

Tarlok Singh

Tarlok Singh designated land as *shahri* (near a city), *neari* (irrigated), *barany* (without irrigation), and in between (land that didn't fall neatly into other categories). A person got more acres if he got *barany* land, and much less if he got *neari* and *shahri* land. Farmers and homeowners had to prove ownership by providing necessary papers. Luckily, the British had established individual ownership rights, and necessary paperwork was available. The government on both sides cooperated in this process.

Under the auspices of the Rehabilitation Act and with the help of some relatives and friends, my extended family was allotted land in a small, established village called Nawan Pind Mehmowala, near the city of Batala, in Gurdaspur district. Before Partition, it had been inhabited solely by Muslims; after they fled, Sikhs were settled there, with the majority of landowners being Chattha Sikh farmers, including my grandfather.

This land was fertile and used irrigation from Persian wells. Unfortunately, our mud houses and crops were frequently destroyed by heavy rains upstream, which caused our land to flood. The government had built a raised railroad line near the village but had built just one opening for drainage. It was completely insufficient. When the floodwaters would reach the raised railroad, water would back up and demolish the mud houses. The railway authorities turned a deaf ear to this problem with the bridge, so villagers would cut more openings in the railway line to save their homes and crops. (Later, to address the flooding, the authorities finally had a canal dug in the late 1950s, which became a waterway called Hansli, over which authorities built a large bridge with many spans.) Today, all the houses in Nawan Pind Mehmowala are brick houses.

Generally, Sikh farmers got less land in east Punjab than they'd had in west Punjab. Some could not sustain their family on the amount of land they'd been allotted, so they bought cheaper and more land in other states of India. Although they felt discriminated against in other states, Punjabi entrepreneurship prevailed. The green revolution, with better seeds and fertilizers, improved the yield of crops.

Even though my family had less land in Nawan Pind Mehmowala than in Pakistan, my people prospered because of education. Now, most of the educated descendants of my great-grandfather have moved away from the village to urban areas and other countries, such as the United States, Canada, Australia, and Great Britain. Also, the village has slowly been encroached upon by nearby Batala. I last visited the village ten years ago and could hardly recognize the people and landscape. I suspect that in the future, it will remain a Chattha village, but the majority of its occupants will be members of other clans.

Look not at the greatness of the evil past, but the greatness of the good to follow

—Thomas Hobbes

Acceptance

In all tragedies, human beings go through Elisabeth Kübler-Ross's stages of denial, anger, bargaining, depression, and, finally, acceptance. The participants of Partition were no different.

There have been many displacements in modern history. A lot has been written about the physical and emotional trauma resulting from the Jewish Holocaust. But little has been written about the trauma of Partition, probably due to a lack of education among its sufferers. My own family moved from place to place in east Punjab before settling, and all this caused some anxiety and depression but no acts of suicide. We were lucky to have some economic cushion from my father's and uncle's stable jobs with the Indian Army.

In general, Punjabis are quite resilient. The migration of 1947 was not a new challenge; for instance, centuries ago we experienced an exodus from Rajasthan and an onslaught by invaders.

In time, my grandfather came to be reconciled to our new situation and no longer talked much against Jinnah, Nehru, or Gandhi. Freedom for him was no longer *barbadi*. His new masters were his own people, and he no longer wanted favors from the British. Deep in his heart, he was happy that free India provided ample opportunity to his grandchildren. One summer I came home from medical school to meet him. I sat with him under the peepal tree where he rested. He appeared quite happy. As a young boy, I had discussed many of my school subjects with him, including the shape of the earth. He used to be very skeptical about the earth being round. Now, after so many years, I wanted to know if he had changed his mind. When I asked, he laughed and jokingly said, "The earth must be round, because we moved to a new village in what is now Pakistan and are back again to the old village. The earth must be round."

As people on both sides of the line of demarcation came to accept their new reality, there was even some renewal of old friendships. For instance, my grandfather's Muslim friend, Sher Mohammed—the only man who called my grandfather by his given name—came to visit him twice in east Punjab. This perhaps showed a return of respect and friendship between those of different religions. At least for a few.

Poems of Partition

The tragedy of the partition of Punjab and Bengal did not go unnoticed by writers. Many novels, short stories, and poems were written by writers on both sides of partitioned Punjab. The same may be true of Bengal. The poems pertaining to Punjab depict an inferno fueled by religion. Poets from India, Pakistan, and Bengal, as well as a few from Britain and the United States, created works in languages including Punjabi, Hindi, Urdu, English, and others. They reference looting and killing as well as the abduction of women—all of which disappeared rather quickly after the migration and religious cleansing were completed. Maybe there were no more left to be killed.

But India is not the only country to experience partition. Many other countries have experienced a division, for instance, Korea, Cyprus, Ireland, Sudan, and many after the fall of the Soviet Union (Hitchens). Where there is pain, there is poetry, and according to the India Seminar, there are more than 500 documented poems related to partitions at various places and at various times in the world (Gupta).

Punjabis will read this poetry with tears and feel remorse for what they did to each other on both sides. With the killings came loss of life, culture, and heritage.

The fire is gone now, leaving for us some smoldering ashes of hatred. Will Phoenix ever rise from these ashes?

Ode to Waris Shah

AMRITA PRITAM (1919–2005)

ENGLISH TRANSLATION

Born Amrit Kaur at Gujranwala, now Pakistan, she is a most beloved and distinguished Punjabi poet. Her poems often describe the plight of women during Partition, and this is her best known poem.

I say to Waris Shah today, speak from your grave And add a
  new page to your book of love
Once one daughter of Punjab wept, and you wrote your long
  saga; Today thousands weep, calling to you Waris Shah:
Arise, o friend of the afflicted; arise and see the state of
  Punjab, Corpses strewn on fields, and the Chenaab
  flowing with much blood.
Someone filled the five rivers with poison, And this same
  water now irrigates our soil.
Where was lost the flute, where the songs of love sounded?
  And all Ranjha's brothers forgotten to play the flute.
Blood has rained on the soil, graves are oozing with
  blood, The princesses of love cry their hearts out in the
  graveyards.

Today all the Quaido'ns have become the thieves of love and
    beauty, Where can we find another one like Waris Shah?
Waris Shah! I say to you, speak from your grave And add a
    new page to your book of love.

PUNJABI

Ajj Akhaan Waris Shah nun
ਅੱਜ ਆਖਾਂ ਵਾਰਸਿ ਸਾਹ ਨੂੰ !

ਅੱਜ ਆਖਾਂ ਵਾਰਸਿ ਸਾਹ ਨੂੰ ਕਿਤੋਂ ਕਬਰਾਂ ਵਿਚੋਂ ਬੋਲ !
ਤੇ ਅੱਜ ਕਿਤਾਬੇ-ਇਸ਼ਕ ਦਾ ਕੋਈ ਅਗਲਾ ਵਰਕਾ ਫੋਲ !
ਇਕ ਰੋਈ ਸੀ ਧੀ ਪੰਜਾਬ ਦੀ ਤੂੰ ਲਿਖਿ ਲਿਖਿ ਮਾਰੇ ਵੈਣ
ਅੱਜ ਲੱਖਾਂ ਧੀਆਂ ਰੋਂਦੀਆਂ ਤੈਨੂੰ ਵਾਰਸਿ ਸਾਹ ਨੂੰ ਕਹਿਣ
ਉਠ ਦਰਦਮੰਦਾਂ ਦਿਆ ਦਰਦਦੀਆ ! ਉਠ ਤੱਕ ਅਪਣਾ ਪੰਜਾਬ
ਅੱਜ ਬੇਲੇ ਲਾਸ਼ਾਂ ਵਿਛੀਆਂ ਤੇ ਲਹੂ ਦੀ ਭਰੀ ਚਨਾਬ
ਕਿਸੇ ਨੇ ਪੰਜਾਂ ਪਾਣੀਆਂ ਵਿਚ ਦਿੱਤੀ ਜ਼ਹਿਰਿ ਰਲਾ
ਤੇ ਉਹਨਾ ਪਾਣੀਆਂ ਧਰਤ ਨੂੰ ਦਿੱਤਾ ਪਾਣੀ ਲਾ
ਇਸ ਜ਼ਰਖੇਜ਼ ਜ਼ਮੀਨ ਦੇ ਲੂੰ ਲੂੰ ਫੁਟਿਆ ਜ਼ਹਰਿ
ਗਿਠਿ ਗਿਠਿ ਚੜ੍ਹੀਆਂ ਲਾਲੀਆਂ ਫੁੱਟ ਫੁੱਟ ਚੜ੍ਹਿਆ ਕਹਰਿ
ਵਹਿ ਵਲੀਸੀ ਵਾ ਫਿਰਿ ਵਣ ਵਣ ਵੱਗੀ ਜਾ
ਉਹਨੇ ਹਰ ਇਕ ਵਾਂਸ ਦੀ ਵੰਝਲੀ ਦਿੱਤੀ ਨਾਗ ਬਣਾ
ਪਹਿਲਾ ਡੰਗ ਮਦਾਰੀਆਂ ਮੰਤਰ ਗਏ ਗੁਆਚ
ਦੂਜੇ ਡੰਗ ਦੀ ਲੱਗ ਗਈ ਜਣੇ ਖਣੇ ਨੂੰ ਲਾਗ
ਲਾਗਾਂ ਕੀਲੇ ਲੋਕ ਮੂੰਹ ਬੱਸ ਫਿਰਿ ਡੰਗ ਹੀ ਡੰਗ
ਪਲੋ ਪਲੀ ਪੰਜਾਬ ਦੇ ਨੀਲੇ ਪੈ ਗਏ ਅੰਗ...
ਗਲਿਓਂ ਟੁੱਟੇ ਗੀਤ ਫਿਰਿ ਤਰਕਲਿਓਂ ਟੁੱਟੀ ਤੰਦ
ਤ੍ਰਿੰਜਣੇ ਟੁੱਟੀਆਂ ਸਹੇਲੀਆਂ ਚਰੱਖੜੇ ਘੂਕਰ ਬੰਦ

ਸਣੇ ਸੇਜ਼ ਤੇ ਬੇੜੀਆਂ ਲੁੱਡਣ ਦਿੱਤੀਆਂ ਰੋੜ੍ਹ
ਸਣੇ ਡਾਲੀਆਂ ਪੀਂਘ ਅੱਜ ਪੀਪਲਾਂ ਦਿੱਤੀ ਤੋੜ੍ਹ
ਜਿਥੇ ਵਜਦੀ ਸੀ ਢੁਕ ਪਿਆਰ ਦੀ ਵੇ ਉਹ ਵੰਝਲੀ ਗਈ ਗੁਆਚ
ਰਾਂਝੇ ਦੇ ਸਭ ਵੀਰ ਅੱਜ ਭੁੱਲ ਗਏ ਉਸਦੀ ਜਾਚ...
ਧਰਤੀ ਤੇ ਲਹੂ ਵੱਸਿਆ ਕਬਰਾਂ ਪਈਆਂ ਚੋਣ
ਪ੍ਰੀਤ ਦੀਆਂ ਸਾਹਜਾਦੀਆਂ ਅੱਜ ਵਿੱਚ ਮਜਾਰਾਂ ਰੋਣ...
ਅੱਜ ਸੱਭੇ ਕੈਦੋ ਬਣ ਗਏ, ਹੁਸਨ ਇਸ਼ਕ ਦੇ ਚੋਰ
ਅੱਜ ਕਬਿੇ ਲਿਆਈਏ ਲੱਭ ਕੇ ਵਾਰਸਿ ਸ਼ਾਹ ਇਕ ਹੋਰ...
ਅੱਜ ਆਖਾਂ ਵਾਰਸਿ ਸ਼ਾਹ ਨੂੰ ਕਿਤੋ ਕਬਰਾਂ ਵਿਚੋਂ ਬੋਲ !
ਤੇ ਅੱਜ ਕਿਤਾਬੇ ਇਸ਼ਕ ਦਾ ਕੋਈ ਅਗਲਾ ਵਰਕਾ ਫੋਲ !

My Punjab Committed Suicide Long Ago

SURJIT PATAR (1945–)

PUNJABI

ਮੇਰੇ ਪੰਜਾਬ ਨੇ ਤਾਂ ਬਹੁਤ ਚਿਰ ਹੋਇਆ ਖ਼ੁਦਕੁਸ਼ੀ ਕਰ ਲਈ ਸੀ
ਤੇ ਉਸ ਦੇ ਪੰਜਾਬੀਆਂ ਵਿੱਚੋਂ ਕੋਈ ਆਇਤ, ਸ਼ਬਦ ਕੋਈ
ਸੀ ਲਿਖਿਆ ਇਸ ਤਰ੍ਹਾਂ ਮਿਲਿਆ:
ਮੇਰੀ ਹੱਤਿਆ ਕਿਸੇ ਹੱਥੋਂ ਨਹੀਂ ਹੋਈ
ਮੈਂ ਆਤਮਘਾਤ ਕੀਤਾ ਹੈ
ਤੇ ਮੇਰੀ ਮੌਤ ਦਾ ਮਾਤਮ ਕਰਨ ਦਾ ਹਕ ਹੈ
ਕੇਵਲ ਹਵਾਵਾਂ ਨੂੰ

ਪੁਰਾ ਵਰਦਾ, ਵਗੇ ਪੱਛੋਂ
ਪੁਰਾ ਪੱਛੋਂ ਦੇ ਗਲ ਲਗ ਕੇ ਜਦੋਂ ਵਿਰਲਾਪ ਕਰਦਾ ਹੈ
ਤਾਂ ਸੀਮਾ 'ਤੇ ਖੜ੍ਹਾ ਸੈਨਿਕ
ਜਾਂ ਸਰਹੱਦ 'ਤੇ ਖੜ੍ਹਾ ਫ਼ੌਜੀ ਹਵਾਂ ਵਿੱਚ ਫ਼ਾਇਰ ਕਰਦਾ ਹੈ
ਤਾਂ ਬਿਰਖਾਂ ਤੋਂ ਤ੍ਰਭਕ ਪੰਛੀ ਅਰਸ਼ ਵਿੱਚ ਸਰਜ ਲਭਦੇ ਨੇ
ਹਵਾ ਰੁੱਖਾਂ ਦੇ ਅੱਥਰੂ ਪੁੰਝਦੀ ਹੈ, ਸਿਸਕਦੀ ਹੈ:
ਮੇਰਾ ਕਾਤਿਲ ਨਹੀਂ ਕੋਈ
ਮੇਰੀ ਹੱਤਿਆ ਕਿਸੇ ਹੱਥੋਂ ਨਹੀਂ ਹੋਈ
ਮੈਂ ਆਤਮਘਾਤ ਕੀਤਾ ਹੈ
ਕਦੀ ਜਦ ਰੇਡੀਓ ਲਾਹੌਰ ਤੋਂ ਕੋਈ ਗੀਤ ਸੁਣਦਾ ਹਾਂ
ਤਾਂ ਮੈਨੂੰ ਜਾਪਦਾ ਹੈ
ਪੁਰ ਪੱਛੋਂ ਦੇ ਗਲ ਲਗ ਰੋ ਰਿਹਾ ਹੈ
ਅਚਾਨਕ ਆਪਣੇ ਹੱਥਾਂ' ਤੇ ਸੁਹੇ ਦਾਗ ਦਿਸਦੇ ਨੇ
ਕਦੀ ਜਦ ਦੇਸ਼ ਦੇ ਰਖਵਾਲਿਆਂ ਨੂੰ ਵਾਜ ਪੈਂਦੀ
ਜਾਂ ਵਤਨ ਦੇ ਗਾਜ਼ੀਆਂ ਨੂੰ ਕੂਕ ਸੁਣਦੀ ਹੈ
ਤਾਂ ਮੈਨੂੰ ਸਮਝ ਨਹੀਂ ਪੈਂਦੀ
ਮੈਂ ਗਾਜ਼ੀ ਹਾਂ ਕਿ ਰਖਵਾਲਾ

ਭਲਾ ਮੈਂ ਵੀ ਇਹ ਕਿਹੜੇ ਕਿੱਸਿਆਂ ਨੂੰ ਛੇੜ ਬੈਠਾ ਹਾਂ
ਮੁਬਾਰਕ ਦਿਵਸ ਹੈ ਆਵੋ
ਨੱਵੇਂ ਪੰਜਾਬ ਦੀ ਦੀਰਘ ਉਮਰ ਲਈ ਵੰਦਨਾ ਕਰੀਏ
ਇਸ ਦੀ ਸਰਹੱਦ 'ਤੇ ਝੰਡਾ ਝੁਲਾ ਦਈਏ

ਕਿਸੇ ਜਾਸੂਸ ਵਾਂਗੀ ਸੁਣ ਸਕਣ ਜੋ ਕੀ ਕੁਸਕਦੇ ਨੇ
ਜਦੋਂ ਪੱਛੋਂ ਤੇ ਪੁਰਵਈਆ ਗਲੇ ਲਗ ਕੇ ਡੁਸਕਦੇ ਨੇ।

In That Direction

SURJIT PATAR (1945–)

ਉਸ ਬੰਨੇ ਸੁਹਣਾ-ਜਿਹਾ ਵਸਦਾ ਗਰਾਂ ਸੀ
ਪਿੱਪਲਾਂ ਤੇ ਬੋਹੜਾ ਨਿੰਮਾਂ ਟਾਹਲੀਆਂ ਦੀ ਛਾਂ ਸੀ

ਰਾਹਵਾਂ ਉੱਤੇ ਸਾਡੇ ਨਿੱਕੇ ਪੈਰਾਂ ਦੀਆਂ ਪੈੜਾਂ ਸਨ
ਦਰਾਂ ਚ ਖਲੋ ਕੇ ਮਾਵਾਂ ਮੰਗਦੀਆਂ ਖ਼ੈਰਾਂ ਸਨ
ਰਾਮਾ ਗਾਮਾ ਜੀਤਾ ਮੇਰੇ ਆੜੀਆਂ ਦੇ ਨਾਂ ਸੀ

ਕਹਿਰ ਦੀਆਂ ਐਸੀਆਂ ਹਨੇਰੀਆਂ ਸੀ ਝੁੱਲੀਆਂ
ਬੰਦਿਆਂ ਦੀ ਛੱਡ ਉਥੇ ਕੌਮਾਂ ਰਾਹਵਾਂ ਭੁੱਲੀਆਂ
ਪੁੱਤ ਕਿੱਥੇ ਰਾਹ ਭੁੱਲੇ ਰੋਂਦੀ ਕਿੱਥੇ ਮਾਂ ਸੀ

ਹਰ ਬੰਦੇ ਵਿੱਚੋਂ ਕੋਈ ਨਿੱਕਲਿਆ ਹੋਰ ਸੀ
ਬੜਾ ਉਥੇ ਮਜ਼ਬਾਂ ਤੇ ਧਰਮਾਂ ਦਾ ਸ਼ੋਰ ਸੀ
ਰੱਬ ਦਾ ਤਾਂ ਉਥੇ ਕਿਤੇ ਨਾਂ ਨਾ ਨਿਸ਼ਾਂ ਸੀ
ਪਾਗਲਾ ਤੂੰ ਰੋਨਾਂ ਏਂ ਕਿ ਪੈੜਾਂ ਮਿਟ ਗਈਆਂ ਨੇ
ਝੱਖੜ ਸੀ ਏਦਾਂ ਦਾ ਕਿ ਰਾਹਵਾਂ ਉੱੜ ਗਈਆਂ ਨੇ
ਅੰਨ੍ਹੇ ਹੋ ਗਏ ਬੰਦੇ ਕੋਈ ਧੀ ਸੀ ਨਾਂ ਮਾਂ ਸੀ

ਰੂਹ ਸਾਡੀ ਉਥੇ ਰਹਿ ਗਈ, ਪਲ ਬੜੇ ਥੋੜ੍ਹੇ ਸੀ
ਜਾਨਾਂ ਹੀ ਬਚਾ ਕੇ ਅਸੀਂ ਮਸੀਂ ਉਥੋਂ ਦੌੜੇ ਸੀ
ਰੱਖਾਂ ਨਾਲੋਂ ਛਾਵਾਂ ਟੁੱਟ ਜਾਣ ਦਾ ਸਮਾਂ ਸੀ

ਹਾਲੇ ਵੀ ਤਾਂ ਪਿੰਡ ਸਾਡਾ ਵੱਸਦਾ ਈ ਹੋਵੇਗਾ
ਸਾਡੇ ਬਾਰੇ ਗੱਲਾਂਬਾਤਾਂ ਦੱਸਦਾ ਈ ਹੋਵੇਗਾ
ਉਹ ਏਥੋਂ ਚਲੇ ਗਏ ਜਿਨ੍ਹਾਂ ਦੀ ਇਹ ਥਾਂ ਸੀ

ਜਦੋਂ ਕਦੀ ਮਿਲਾਂਗੇ ਤਾਂ ਸੀਨੇ ਲੱਗ ਰੋਣਗੇ
ਵਿਹੜਿਆਂ ਦੇ ਰੁੱਖ ਵੀ ਉਡੀਕਦੇ ਤਾਂ ਹੋਣਗੇ
ਜਿਨ੍ਹਾਂ ਦਿਆਂ ਤਣਿਆਂ ਤੇ ਖੁਭੇ ਅਸਾਂ ਨਾਂ ਸੀ॥

Milk Got Cracked

ATAL BIHARI VAJPAYEE (1924–)

ENGLISH TRANSLATION

A former Prime Minister of India, Vajpayee is also a poet.

Why blood turned white?
Lost the similarity in the difference,
Martyr got divided, the songs got short,
Dagger got into the chest,
Milk got cracked.

Smell of gunpowder in the fields,
verses of Nanak are broken,
river Satluj got terrified, the state is in distress,
Spring turned to Fall.
Milk got cracked.

hate from own shadow,
the strangers are hugging,
the path of suicide, vow to you of your country,
the order has vanished.
Milk got cracked.

दूध में दरार पड़ गई

HINDI

खून क्यों सफेद हो गया?

भेद में अभेद खो गया।
बंट गये शहीद, गीत कट गए,
कलेजे में कटार दड़ गई।
दूध में दरार पड़ गई।

खेतों में बारूदी गंध,
टूट गये नानक के छंद।
सतलुज सहम उठी, व्यथित सी बितस्ता है।
वसंत से बहार झड़ गई।
दूध में दरार पड़ गई।

अपनी ही छाया से बैर,
गले लगने लगे हैं ग़ैर,
खुदकुशी का रास्ता, तुम्हें वतन का वास्ता।
बात बनाएं, बिगड़ गई।
दूध में दरार पड़ गई।

MOHAN SINGH (1905–1978)
He was a pioneer of modern Punjabi poetry. The lines below are
an extract from a lengthier poem.

PUNJABI

ਆ ਬਾਬਾ ਤੇਰਾ ਵਤਨ ਹੈ ਵੀਰਾਨ ਹੋ ਗਿਆ
ਰੱਬ ਦੇ ਘਰਾਂ ਦਾ ਰਾਖਾ ਮੁੜ ਸ਼ੈਤਾਨ ਹੋ ਗਿਆ

ਵੰਡ ਬੈਠੇ ਤੇਰੇ ਪੁੱਤ ਨੇ ਸਾਂਝੇ ਸਵਰਗ ਨੂੰ
ਵੰਡਿਆ ਸਵਰਗ ਨਰਕ ਦਾ ਸਾਮਾਨ ਹੋ ਗਿਆ

ਕੁੱਝ ਐਸਾ ਕੁਫਰ ਤੋਲਿਆ ਈਮਾਨ ਵਾਲਿਆਂ
ਕਿ ਕੁਫਰ ਤੋਂ ਵੀ ਹੋਲਾ ਹੈ ਈਮਾਨ ਹੋ ਗਿਆ

Poetry is part of Punjabi culture—both in the past and currently. You
can find the more famous poems on Youtube or in books; less well-
known poems can be heard at *Mushaira* (poetry symposia, where
poets and listeners gather to hear poems performed) in northern
India and Pakistan.

In addition to the poets quoted on previous pages, other of note
include the following:

Indian Poets
Shailendra (1923–1966). Born Shankardas Kesarilal at
   Rawalpindi, West Punjab (now Pakistan), he wrote poems
   for many Indian movies. His famous poem regarding
   Partition is Jalta Hai Punjab. He narrated at a poetry
   symposium.

Shiv Batalvi (1937–1973). A most outstanding Punjabi poet, he was born at the village of Bara pind lohtian, Tehsil Shakar garh, District Sialkot. He was my contemporary at Sikh National College at Qadian District, Gurdaspur, East Punjab. His famous poem regarding partition is *Dudh da Qatal* (Murder of Mother's Milk).

Pakistani Poets

Ahmed Rahi (1923–2002) (described the suffering of girls during Partition in his book *Trinjhann*)

Afzal Saahir (born in Lahore, his famous poem about partition is "Ujhaarha [Refugee])

Bengali Poets

Jibanananda Das (1899–1954) (poems include "Go Where You Will" and "I Have Seen Bengali's Face")

Taslima Nasrin (1962–) (the poet, physician, and women's rights activist's poems include "Broken Bengal" and "Denial")

Urdu Poets

Many outstanding Urdu poets have been compiled in the book *Looking Back: The 1947 Partition of India, 70 Years On.* Poets featured include the following:

Ahmad Nadeem Qasmi ("Phir Achanak Teergi Mein Aa Gae")

Asrarul Haq Majaz ("Inquilab [Revolution]")

Faiz Ahmed Faiz ("Subah e azaadi")

Ali Sardar Jafri ("Subh e Farda")
Josh Malihabadi ("Matam e Azadi")
Akhtarul Iman ("Pandrah Agust")
Sardar Jafri ("Gufatgu" and "Dushmankaun")

English Poets

W. H. Auden (1907–1973) (wrote about Cyril Radcliffe
  making the boundary line without mentioning his name)
Moniza Alvi (of Pakistani origin, she wrote a book of 20
  poems)

American Poet

Poet Marya Mannes (1904–1990) (poet and critic, she wrote
  about partitions in general)

The Consequences of the Migration

Every forced migration has emotional and material impact, and Partition was no exception. The refugees suffered in many ways, some for a lifetime. The effects of the lengthy journey, undertaken without warning or preparation, include the following:

Material loss. In this hurried migration, families lost land, homes and belongings, animal stock, and many other precious things. For instance, my grandfather raised horses in Chattha Chak No. 46 and was proud to show off medals awarded to him. All those were left behind. Valuable family photographs were left behind as well.

Loss of loved ones. Some were left behind and forced to embrace Islam. Some died during the journey from Muslim bandits, starvation, accidents, or diseases such as cholera.

Social stigma. Early on, displaced persons were considered second-class citizens. They were called *sharnarthies* and *panaghazeers* (refugees). There was some discrimination even at the matrimonial level.

Psychological and emotional loss. The loss of birthplace meant, for some, the loss of family identity built over generations. Further, leaving behind Gurdwaras and shrines meant a disconnect from centers of religious life.

Most refugees suffered anxiety and depression from uncertainty regarding food, personal safety, and the future. Psychiatric services were, of course, nonexistent, and no statistics were gathered regarding mental health among the refugees. No health care data was collected from that time, including suicide rates.

Part 5

Connection and Heritage

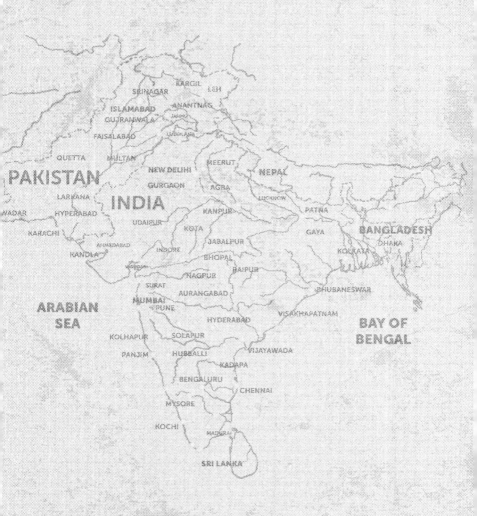

Gulam Heather Chattha
and His Search for Another Chattha

About twenty years ago, I met a distant uncle named Gulam Heather Chattha. At the time, he was in his mid-sixties, and I was a few years younger.

Gulam Heather, a Muslim, had moved from Chattha Chak No. 46 and was living with his son and daughter, their spouses, and a few grandchildren in Toronto. Once Gulam Heather had settled in Canada, he began searching for other Chatthas in the telephone directory. Toronto has a large Indian and Pakistani community, and he thought he might find a Chattha relative living there. Was he looking for a Muslim Chattha or *any* Chattha? Was he curious or homesick for his clan? I do not know. In any case, he found in the phone book a Manjit Singh Chattha living in Mississauga, Ontario. Gulam Heather Chattha was certain Manjit Chattha had his roots in Chattha Chak No. 46, so, excitedly, he called him. Their conversation was brief, and Manjit went to see him after a couple of days.

Gulam Heather had not thought there were other Sikh Chatthas in east Punjab except the ones living in Gurdaspur district, their ancestral village. When they spoke, Gulam Heather was anxious to learn if Manjit Singh had an ancestral connection to Chattha Chak No. 46 and was thrilled when he learned he did. It turned out that Gulam Heather had known Manjit Singh's father, my uncle S. Shingara Singh Chattha. He also had known my late elder brother, Harbans Chattha. He inquired at length about our whole, extended family. A door was open now for more conversation and socialization between Gulam Heather and my entire family.

When my cousin Manjit related to me his conversation with Gulam Heather, I knew I had to meet him. He was a link to a time and place left behind. What could he tell me about my village? About the people who remained? About how my home had changed? So in 1995, I, along with my wife, traveled from West Virginia to Toronto to meet him. We spent an afternoon together and had a cup of tea. When his daughter served tea, she addressed me as *bhaji* (brother). He was happy and proud to know that I was a neurologist in the United States and that my elder brother, Ajit Singh, had been chief secretary to the government of Punjab.

A few months later, I made a second trip to Toronto to see him. When I arrived at his home, his daughter told me he was at a nearby park. I drove to the park and walked to an area where a few people were sitting under a tree. Four of them were playing cards: three elderly, turbaned Sikhs and Gulam Heather, the only Muslim. All four were Punjabis, from two separate countries. As I approached, he put his cards down and stood up. He addressed his companions: "Please meet my nephew. He is the most famous neurologist in USA. People all over come to see him. Oh, and his older brother, my nephew Ajit Singh Chattha, is the governor of east Punjab." One elderly Sikh in the group corrected him, "Chief secretary, not governor." He replied, "It is one and the same thing." Why he went out of his way to shower praise I do not know except it was from deep inner love and pride. Two different countries and two different religions, but the same clan.

I enjoyed every moment of this meeting, so I made a third trip to Toronto, this time meeting him at home. We talked about his wife's poor health. He told me he had been practicing medicine at home in Pakistan but did not have a medical degree. (During the era of his adulthood, it was fairly common in both India and Pakistan to have registered medical practitioners who lacked proper training.) In Chattha Chak No. 46, he had tried every medicine to help his wife, but she remained weak and pale. He suggested he might bring his wife to me in the United States for treatment. We talked about other things, but he appeared depressed. I ventured to ask him if he was happy in Canada.

He said, "All is well, but I am worried about my grandchildren. These children will forget everything about Islam."

I said, "You know there is a big mosque nearby?"

"I know, but it is not the same thing as in Pakistan," he said.

I commented, "But Quran and teaching should be the same at any mosque."

"Well, maybe. But at this mosque, there are people from many countries, and only few can speak Punjabi and all that. Amrik, I am seriously thinking of taking my grandchildren to Pakistan."

His daughter had been listening in kitchen, making tea for us. She spoke from the kitchen, "*Bhaji*, please fix *Abba*'s [father's] brain." I commented to my new friend, "The kids will have a better life, more education, better jobs, bigger homes, and cars in Canada. Why take them back to Pakistan?" He kept quiet. I also dared to say, with a laugh, that his grandsons might get married to beautiful local girls. He became upset and said, "Even you are taking her side."

I changed the conversation to something I had been wondering about for many years. Since Gulam Heather had continued to live in Chak No. 46, I thought he might know the answer to a question that had haunted our family since that chaotic time just before we joined the *kafla*. "Who," I asked him, "killed Uncle Inder Singh and Arjan Singh?" He paused to think about it—so many years had passed—and then gave the name Ditto, a man who apparently had lived in our village. With that one word, a family pain, a family mystery, finally had an answer. Though so many questions about Partition remain unanswered, now our family at least had this one closure.

According to Gulam Heather, Ditto had lingered on his deathbed for some time, suffering. He said to those around him, repeatedly, that he felt he was being punished for killing Inder Singh and Arjan Singh, and he begged for forgiveness from Allah.

Gulam Heather felt sad about Partition and all its consequences. He told me that, in 1947, as my family fled the village, refugees from United Province of India (now Uttar Pradesh) had occupied our houses and land. These newcomers brought with them a different language and culture. The Village Chattha, he said, is not the same now as before Partition.

Wishing to lighten the mood, I suggested to Gulam Heather that I might want to visit the place of my birth. His eyes brightened and his mood changed. "Sure," he said. "I will send your *chachi* [aunt] ahead of your visit, and she will take care of you." (By *chachi* he meant his wife, who though in poor health was able to get around.) Later that year, in 1997, Jaswinder and I with a small group of friends were able to visit Pakistan. Gulam Heather and his wife had attended to our trip with passion, and, sure enough, Gulam Heather's wife was waiting for us in Chak No. 46. In the village, I saw the sign on his house: "Dr. Gulam Heather Chattha." After the visit, I called him in Toronto to thank him.

Unfortunately, for the past two years, as I've been writing this book, I have been unable to reach him or his children at their last telephone number and postal address. Maybe he left for Pakistan or was a victim of old age and ill health.

This story has deep meaning to me. Gulam Heather Chattha loved Punjabiat. He had pride in being a Chattha—whether Sikh or Muslim. India and Pakistan were not barriers to his feelings.

Still, Islam was part of his soul. Despite his feelings for Punjabiat, the teachings of Islam were a priority in his mind so far as his grandchildren were concerned. He struggled to reconcile the opportunities offered to his grandchildren in Canada with the threat to Islam he perceived in the West. These issues were challenging to him at his age.

THERE ARE OTHER examples of mutual love among Punjabis. One that comes to mind was a trip I made to China in 2002. I was traveling with a group, and we were at the Beijing airport when two young Pakistani businessmen, from Gujranwala, noticed my turban and recognized me as a Punjabi. They were gracious enough to come over and introduce themselves to me. They thought I must be the head of a visiting *wafad* (delegation). Of course, I explained who I was. They gave me their business cards and invited me to their homes in Pakistan.

Another example is from my trip to Pakistan in 1997. While walking in a bazaar in Rawalpindi, I saw a sign on a shop, "Ludhiana clothes merchant." I went in and asked the young salesman, "Why do you have this sign since your business is in Rawalpindi?" He told me, "This is the original name of the store from when we lived in Ludhiana, and we have proudly kept the name." I told him that a member of our group was from Ludhiana, in east Punjab. He got very excited and said, "I am calling my dad. He'll be overjoyed to see you and the man from Ludhiana." In the meantime, he ordered tea for us.

Yet another example of Punjabiat from that same trip: while waiting in line at a ticket window at Islamabad, an airline executive walked over and told me, "*Sardar Sahib* [dear sir], you are our guest; hence you need not wait in line." Then he got me a priority boarding pass. What a change in a few years! Not long ago my family had been chased out of Pakistan, and now I was being given special favors from one Punjabi brother to another. This is Punjabiat at its best.

These are just some examples of Punjabiat I've experienced over the years that override geographical and religious boundaries. I have wondered whether I got this respect only because I was a guest. Would things have been different if I had decided to live in Pakistan permanently? I also wonder if polling were done today, how many Punjabis would vote in favor of uniting Punjab again.

....

Punjabiat. It is the changing physical and cultural construct of people living in Punjab. They are handsome, hardworking, and entrepreneurial. They are brave, kind, and happy-go-lucky. They are eager to serve with humility and cannot tolerate arrogance and injustice.

—Amrik Singh Chattha

....

My Trip to Pakistan:
A Pilgrimage to My Birthplace

I have always had a desire to visit the place of my birth and early upbringing; however, I was busy with my studies, medical training, family, and establishing and building my medical practice in the United States. Also, for many decades, Pakistan was too unstable and was hostile to non-Muslim travelers.

In 1967, Jaswinder and I, with our child, moved to the United States, and I ended up practicing neurology in Weirton, a small town near Pittsburgh, Pennsylvania, in 1974. Down the Ohio River about thirty miles, in Wheeling, West Virginia, was a group of physicians from Pakistan. We became friends and socialized, and we often talked about growing up in West Punjab. I mentioned to them that I had a desire to visit my birthplace. One of them had a close relative in charge of private security for the prime minister of Pakistan, and this physician friend made arrangements with his relative for a group of us to visit Pakistan. That is how, in 1997, our group of eight, all living in or near Wheeling, West Virginia, were able to make a comfortable and safe trip to Pakistan. Our group consisted

Amrik with his Muslim kin in his home village, Chattha Chak No. 46, now located in Pakistan. Amrik is in the center in the dark shirt; Jaswinder is on the far left, with Gulam Heather Chattha's wife standing next to her.

At the National Mosque, in Islamabad: (from left) Amrik Chattha, Teji Bhuller, Jaswinder Chattha, Satinder Bhuller, Nafisa Din, Pete Sandhu, Shivtej Sandhu, and Jagtar Sandhu.

At the home of the parents of Nuzat Saeed in a suburb of Islamabad:
(from left) Shivtej Sandhu, Jaswinder Chattha, Amrik Chattha, Nuzat Saeed's
mother, Satinder Bhuller, Nuzat Saeed's father, Pete Sandhu, Nuzat Saeed, Nafisa
Din, Saeed Iqbal, Teji Bhuller, and Jagtar Sandhu.

In the village of Satinder Bhuller's maternal grandparents, in Pakistan: (from left)
Amrik Chattha, Jagtar Sandhu, Satinder Bhuller (in glasses), and Teji Bhuller
(standing, with teacup in hand) with some people of the village.

Visitors and host families at the Marriot Hotel in Islamabad.

Jaswinder Chattha smiles from the door of a typical bus in Pakistan with the body painted and decorated in floral and geometric designs.

Amrik Chattha contemplates a wall of the home where he was born, in Chattha Chak No. 46, now in Pakistan.

of Jaswinder and me, two other Indian couples, the twenty-two-year-old son of one couple, and the wife of the Pakistani physician who arranged the trip. Our hosts in Pakistan, well connected politically and descendants of big landlords, had many family members living abroad, so they had been exposed to Western culture. They were friendly and tolerant—not religious zealots. They were more than willing to host us.

In the late nineties, Pakistan was quite peaceful for tourists. Three of us traveling were Jat Sikhs born in west Punjab, and we all had fond memories of our early childhood.

Jaswinder and I had applied for visas a few months before the scheduled trip. For two months, there was no response from the Pakistan consulate. We got concerned. A Sikh with a turban on his passport could be a red flag, so maybe the background checks were holding up the process. Before buying the airline ticket, I wanted to be sure we would be granted travel visas.

Apparently, my turban was not the problem. The official in charge of visas had been on vacation, resulting in the delay. (In the past, I had a similar experience with the Indian embassy, but things have improved now.) Once we had our visas in hand, we bought tickets and booked our luggage direct to Islamabad, in Pakistan.

Before our journey, we had asked one of our hosts if there was a gift we could bring for him. To our surprise, he asked for a dozen bottles of scotch, which we carried on our flight in a rolling suitcase.

Alcohol is banned in the Islamic Republic, and drinking alcohol is against the tenets of Islam. One Muslim friend told me that the prophet Mohammed banned alcohol because people would become more argumentative and quarrelsome after drinking. I thought, "Maybe alcohol is okay for our hosts," who were well behaved and civilized.

On the day of our trip, when we got to JFK, in New York City, we saw that while we carried our handbags and alcohol, other passengers were carrying cooking utensils and other household goods from the West to their home country. From JFK, we flew to Heathrow, in London, and then on to Islamabad. When we landed in Pakistan, the weather was good with a nice March breeze. Excitement was in air. Our luggage, however, did not arrive when we did. (When it finally came, the next day, the suitcases were ripped and many valuables had been stolen.)

Going through immigration was a nonevent, but we were stopped at customs. They unzipped and searched our carry-on bags. What is in this suitcase? Scotch? The custom employees were happy with this catch. The boss was called, and he looked at us. "Alcohol is a no-no in Pakistan," he explained, "and the punishment is jail." I argued, "We are on a sightseeing trip." One junior employee, in a bribery attempt, said, "Fifty dollars per bottle will do." Our excitement changed to anxiety and perspiration. A Muslim friend, who had traveled with us from West Virginia, told the customs people, "These people are VIP." Soon a dozen people appeared at the airport and put garlands around our necks, shouting, "Welcome to Pakistan!" This confirmed our VIP status, and soon we were scot-free though scotch-free. State vehicles took us to our host's home, with our luggage to follow. We had high tea, and the men went to a room for scotch, ice, and *nukal* (snacks). The door was closed. Only servants were allowed. Women were forbidden to be part of this secret cocktail party. Jaswinder and the other women went to a separate room with the lady of the house.

After a few drinks, our host bragged about the future of Pakistan, his resource-rich country with acres of flat, irrigated land and a large mine of rock salt. He did not know much about industry and trade. We all nodded yes to everything he said and avoided any talk about Kashmir. A kebab dinner was followed by dessert, and then we were led to our bedrooms. Our luggage had not yet come. One driver headed to airport to investigate and was told our luggage was still at JFK airport. He left with a promise that the luggage would arrive "tomorrow." Thankfully, our host provided all we needed. I was provided a *salwar* (pajamas) and a *kameez* (shirt). It is rare to wear *salwar kameez* at night in east Punjab, but in west Punjab, it is worn day and night as a national dress.

IT MAY BE of interest to Western readers to know that Punjabi Muslims, Hindus, and Sikhs differ not only in religion, but in other areas as well, such as:

Language. Though West Punjab and East Punjab have different official languages—Urdu and Hindi, respectively—the religions share the same Punjabi language, though each writes in different scripts: Gurmukhi for Sikhs and Hindus, and Shahmukhi for Muslims. In everyday speech, two languages are often used. For instance, some urbanites in West Punjab may use Urdu to address a father (*Abbu*), sister (*Humsera*), or maternal aunt (*Khala*) but in the same conversation address other family members in Punjabi.

Colors. Green is the color for purity in Islam, and yellow or saffron is the color of purity for Hindus and Sikhs.

Turbans. Muslims wear white turbans, which are worn mostly by a preacher or mullah. In the past, a Muslim turban had a *kulla* (stiff cap under the turban), but some men wore a *rumi topi* (cap). All colors are used for Sikh turbans including red, green, and blue. Some Akali Sikhs wore blue turbans, and some Sikhs wore saffron turbans, a Hindu legacy.

Dress. *Salwar kameez* and *achkan* or *sherwani* (knee-length jacket) are worn by Muslims. Shorts, pajamas, and Western clothes are for Hindus and Sikhs. Some politicians in India wear Gandhi *topi*, a white shirt, and pajamas.

Meat. Cow meat is banned for Hindus and Sikhs, but it's a delicacy for Muslims. Muslims sacrifice animals with slow decapitation and bleeding, called *halal*. Sikhs and Hindus decapitate with one stroke, called *jhatka*.

Animal worship. Hindus worship the cow, monkey, cobra, and even the rat.

Alcohol. In Pakistan, alcohol is banned for Muslims but not for Hindus and Sikhs.

Death rituals. Muslims, Christians, and Jews bury their dead, while Hindus and Sikhs cremate.

Smoking. Smoking is banned for Sikhs only. Hookah smoking is more prevalent among Muslims.

Hair. Sikhs keep their hair unshorn. Muslims and Hindus do not keep this custom. Also, Muslim men shave their beards differently than do Sikhs and Hindus and use henna to hide the white hair of aging.

Head and body coverings. Muslim women wear a veil, burka, or hijab.

Crescent with moon. Many Muslim nation flags have a crescent with a moon (a legacy of the Ottoman Empire).

Sacred plants. The tulsi plant (also known as holy basil) is sacred to Hindus but not to Muslims and Sikhs.

Marriage. Marriage among cousins and within the clan is preferred among west Punjab Muslims, while the custom is despised by Sikhs and Hindus.

Circumcision. Male circumcision is still practiced among Muslims and some Jews still on the subcontinent.

Different names for the same God. The names for God include "Allah" for Muslims, "Parmeshar" for Hindus, "Waheguru guru Akal purkh" for Sikhs, and "Rubb," a compromise name for God for all Punjabis. I heard in one country that Muslims objected to use of word "Allah" in a Christian church.

When I was little, growing up in Chak No. 46 in a village of Sikhs and Muslims, I had some idea about the differences in custom and beliefs. During our trip, these differences were more obvious to me. Nowadays, because of education, the differences mentioned above are vanishing, especially in urban areas.

DESPITE THE SCOTCH, I did not get a deep sleep that night. I was worried about our luggage and also had some jet lag. The next day, we did sightseeing of the brand-new, modern city of Islamabad, the capital of Pakistan. The city was built in the foothills, not far from hill station of Murree, a town built by the British to get away from the scorching heat of the plains of Punjab in the summer. We had lunch at a Marriott and visited a country club. At one point, our host pointed to a well-dressed gentleman at a distance and told us the man was a member of the National Assembly and represented many villages of the Chattha clan. He was well educated and owned huge land holdings. Pakistan is a feudal society, and many poor people work for rich farmers. My host couldn't have cared less about this gentleman because the man belonged to the opposition in the National Assembly.

After a nice sleep, the next day we headed to a Sikh shrine called Panja Sahib, located at Hasan Abdal. There, the authorities at the entrance of the Gurdwara took our passports, and we were led in. Our hosts were not allowed. Apparently, Muslims cannot go to others' religious places in Pakistan. During our brief trip to Panja Sahib, we were accompanied by two college students. For the sake of curiosity, I asked those young girls if they knew about Sikhism. They were ignorant about Sikhs even though at one time, Sikhs constituted a significant part of Pakistan population. They told me frankly that books and literature about other religions are banned in school and in the college curricula in the Islamic Republic. They were surprised to see my turban, which was different from the one worn by Muslim clerics.

A few years later, one of those college students and her mother visited me in the United States. She wanted me to help her locate geographic east and west. For a moment, I was puzzled by her request. Then she clarified: she wanted to know the proper direction for her *namaz* (prayer). She probably wanted to face in the direction of Mecca. A few months later, she had a brief marriage to a cousin, which resulted in divorce. After that, she lived and worked alone in Manhattan, in New York City. She visited me a few years later, and I wondered whether she would again ask for east and west directions. But this time, she did not do any *namaz*. Maybe she thought that prayer had not helped her in life. Or maybe living in a multicultural and multireligious society in the United States changed her thinking.

From Islamabad, our party flew to Lahore. The clerk at the ticket counter had a story to tell me. He said, "Sardar Sahib, did you see a big *jaloose* [procession] of vehicles carrying green flags? In the vehicle in front of this procession is a Sikh convert to Islam, and this function is in his honor." I kept quiet. Islam believes in conversions and honors converts. I muttered in a low tone, "Good for Sardar Ji." I know of some Sikh converts to Christianity. During Raj they were sent for higher studies to England and even married white Anglo-Saxon women.

Religion remains an important part of daily life in Pakistan and the Middle East, while its role is diminishing in other parts of the world.

We landed at Lahore and stayed in a five-star hotel that was once a Hilton franchise. It was a very quiet place with no bar. One hotel employee arranged some scotch for us. Alcohol is not banned for non-Muslims, and Pakistan had a brewery for them.

Lahore is a remarkable city and was once considered the heart of undivided Punjab, the center of higher education, commerce, and entertainment. It has historic buildings, Mughal architecture, and museums. It was the birthplace of the Indian movie industry, which shifted to Bombay (now Mumbai) after 1947 and became Bollywood. Lahore was all fashion and romance. As it was rightly said, *"Sak Maldian Ravi De Kandian Te Ag Loon lahorons Chalian ne."* (Women of Lahore used lipstick from the bark of trees to kindle fire love and romance.) It had the footprints of the Sikh Empire, well described by Amardeep Singh in his book *Lost Heritage: The Sikh Legacy in*

Pakistan. In Lahore, tourists can visit the famous cannon Bhangian di Top, which at the time of the Sikh kingdom was the largest cannon known. In battle, Sikhs defeated a Mughal king in northwest Punjab and took possession of the cannon, which now is located opposite the Institute of Chemical Engineering and Technology, Panjab University. Also called Zamzama or Kims gun, it is mentioned in the writings of Rudyard Kipling. This gun changed hands many times and was once in the hands of a powerful Muslim Chattha clan, who confronted the Sikh emperor Ranjit Singh. The canon is used in Punjabi folklore to deflate others' ego: "Hey, are you Bhangian di Top?" meaning, "Do you think you are as big as Bhangian di Top?" Unfortunately, many other historic objects and manuscripts of the Sikhs' kingdom languish in Pakistan's museums.

On our trip, we enjoyed dinner twice at Salt'n Pepper Village Restaurant in Lahore, which claims to offer the best authentic Punjabi cuisine. A Punjabi singer moved from table to table, entertaining diners with old Punjabi lyrics of the poem "Heer Ranjha." We also enjoyed Punjabi drama at the Alhambra theater near our hotel.

The next side trip took us over to the Nankana Sahib shrine, the birthplace of Guru Nanak, the founder of Sikhism. I was told Guru Nanak was at one time revered by both Hindus and Muslims, each claiming him as their prophet. (One of Guru's companions was a Muslim.) The sanctum sanctorum was riddled with bullets from when Sikhs fought for the control of the shrine from *mahants* (caretakers) during Mughal and British rules.

Jaswinder and I were now getting restless to visit the village of my birth, which was the main objective of our trip. The following day, we headed down a dusty road to my village, Chattha Chak No. 46, not far from Nankana Sahib. Gulam Heather Chattha, whom I'd met in Toronto, had indeed sent his wife from Toronto to Pakistan ahead of our trip to arrange our visit.

My village was close to the small city of Sangla Hill. (The hill is no longer visible; railway authorities hauled away all the stone for railway lines many years ago.) As we approached, I observed that the village appeared backward compared to the villages of east Punjab, and I did not see any cars or tractors. The rich and elite had migrated to urban areas, and those remaining did not appear well educated. However, as we drove up, many villagers appeared to greet us wearing new or newly washed clothes. There was much hugging and handshaking. Love abounds everywhere.

As we walked around the village, I noticed a few things. The Sikh Gurdwara of my childhood had been converted to a school, and the well next door was filled with sand, concrete, and mud. Before Partition, this well had been a bathing place. The village's water had a high fluoride content, which caused the teeth of all the children to look brown. Drinking water was hauled from another well a few hundred yards away. Distant uncle Harnam Singh was the *mashki* (person who distributes water using a sheepskin container), who took water to all the homes. The home where I was raised was now subdivided and beyond recognition. I could not find the room given to my mother to keep her belongings in our large extended family. There was no courtyard, where we had slept in summer and played during the day.

Nobody recognized me. Of course, I was only ten years old when we left that village. Some middle-aged and elderly people talked about my grandfather, father, and uncle, whom they remembered. One middle-aged male had gone to school with my eldest brother, Harbans Singh. We enjoyed a delicious lunch and went from home to home for cups of tea. Some wanted favors from the state, which they thought we might be able to arrange since we were traveling in state vehicles. One gentleman asked if I could take his son to the United States. One elderly man was sobbing and crying. When questioned, he responded, "We miss you. You are our Chattha brothers." He continued:

"There was some jubilation when Sikhs left. We grabbed your land and houses. But soon came the flood of refugees from the Bihar and UP provinces of India, and land and houses were allotted to them. We had culture shock. The newcomers, though Muslim, had different language, food habits, and culture. The Chattha clan was encroached on by others, with no regard for our sisters and daughters. We suffered as much as you did, even though we did not lose our land and homes".

This trip had joy, tears, and sorrow. A meeting like this will never happen again because the actors of this drama will soon be gone forever.

We returned to Lahore late that evening. The next day, we went to the village of my friend Jagtar Sandhu, who was traveling with us along with his wife and son. His father had decent land holdings. Interestingly, the well in the fields was called *billian da khoo* (the well owned by blue-eyed). This village had had an all-Sikh population, which left for India en masse. No one who lived there now knew his family.

The last village we visited belonged to the maternal grandfather of my friend Dr. Satinder Bhuller, also a member of our group. His grandfather had been a rich farmer, and the village was named after his great-grandfather. The children in the family had been taken to a school on a *tonga* (horse-drawn chariot) when they were young and living in the village. Many loyal caretakers of this rich farmer still lived there. One of them had even gone to India and stayed with the family for six months after Partition, before returning home to the village. One man, with tears in his eyes, showed us the place where the rich Sardar Ji had once leisurely walked. This man also showed us some photographs of children well dressed in school uniforms, but

Satinder was unable to recognize any of the children in the photos. We left the village late at night, in darkness, without any fear.

From Lahore, we flew to New Delhi, and a few days later flew back to Islamabad en route to the United States.

On that trip back to my homeland, I learned religion may be important, but culture, language, and Punjabiat are potent forces that bind us together. Long live Punjabiat. Long live my childhood playground.

Part 6

The Neurobiology of Violence

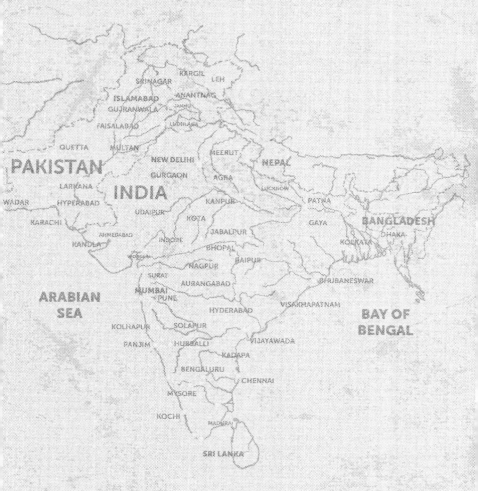

The Neurobiology of Violence

During my training at Massachusetts General Hospital of Harvard Medical School, I became interested in the neurobiology of violence and attended seminars and read literature on the subject, always keeping in mind my own experience of Partition-related violence. Then, as a practicing neurologist, I continued to read, study, and think about the barbarities perpetrated by mobs on people of another religion. I think it important to share with readers the neurobiology of violence in general and the mob violence of Partition in particular. Of course, neurology, biology, genetics, and other scientific areas of study of the body are complex and interconnected, so the information below is simplified. Still, it can shed some light on why group violence occurs. Perhaps neurobiology can begin to answer, in part, some of the "whys" for all the suffering.

THE VIOLENCE OF PARTITION is hardly a unique phenomenon. Not only has violence haunted the entirety of human history—from individual attacks to gang violence to regional skirmishes to world wars—but its roots sprawl also throughout the animal kingdom, of which humans are just a part. For instance, elephants, chimpanzees, wolves, and crows show empathy to their disabled and sick, but as a group they are violent to invading herds and will protect their territory (de Waal). In human beings, aggressiveness appears early. Babies as young as two years old will show love and compassion to their parents, but will also fight for toys, pulling and pushing and even biting. Aggression is evolutionarily built into us, a survival mechanism that traces through our ancestors.

Violent acts committed by individuals can be devastating, but perhaps even worse are violent acts committed as a community or mob, such as the Muslim-on-Sikh violence at the village of Bhulair. Many times skirmishes, riots, wars, even genocides have been triggered by the threat (or perceived threat) posed by competing clans or religions. Think of the Jewish Holocaust, the Rwandan Genocide, the current Buddhist-Muslim (Rohingya) conflict in Myanmar, the Indian Partition, and countless more.

What makes peaceful, loving, and empathetic people become suddenly violent and hateful as happened during Partition? The causes of violence can be attributed to environment, upbringing, personality, and religious beliefs.

The Role of Genetics

Violent tendencies can be passed on in genes, as shown by twin and family studies. Impulsive aggression has a roughly fifty percent chance of being passed on to children (Siever). Genetic predisposition, however, certainly does not explain all aggressive behavior. Surprisingly, according to recent experiments, it appears that the environment can also influence human behavior at the genetic level. This is called behavioral epigenetics (Powledge, Moore). "Epigenetics" refers to chemical changes that change gene *expression* without altering the DNA code. Epigenetics means, essentially, that extra information is layered on DNA (Moore). It is the idea that environmental factors can change the behavior not only of the generation that experiences that environmental stimulus, but also of *future generations*. What does all this mean?

Let me share an experiment conducted by Brian Dias and Kerry Ressler at Emory University that helps explain epigenetics. The researchers made certain mice afraid of a fruity odor by pairing it with a mild shock. Ten days after this fear training began, the researchers allowed the mice to mate and have offspring, which were immediately removed from the cage to eliminate the possibility of learned behavior. Here's the surprising part: the offspring—the *next generation*—exhibited increased sensitivity to the fruity smell even though they had never been exposed the smell before. (They did not react to other smells, only to the fruity smell.) The second generation of mice were allowed to mate, and the third generation of mice also showed an increased sensitivity to the fruity odor (Hughes).

Could epigenetics help explain in part the legacy of generational mistrust, hatred, and violence between groups of people? Could the Muslims, Sikhs, and Hindus of Partition be influenced by a long-ago hatred expressed in their genes?

In *The Other Side of Silence: Voices from the Partition of India,* Urvashi Butalia describes a man raised as a Hindu and converted to Islam after Partition. The man's son, born and raised a Muslim, questions his father's loyalty to the Islamic Republic of Pakistan. The son's antagonistic behavior may be explained on the basis of the prolonged exposure of the young brain to his environment, despite similar genomics of father and the son. In the context of Partition, could identical twins, one raised as Muslim, the other as Hindu or Sikh, hate each other? Yes, and the hatred can be explained, in part, by behavioral epigenetics.

Religious Identity and Profiling

In Punjab during the first half of the twentieth century, it was a fairly simple matter to identify who belonged to what religion. For instance, there were physical markers to identify *us* and *them* such as circumcision (practiced only by Muslims, since Jews were nearly nonexistent in Punjab), religious tatoos, ornaments (bindis), and religious practices (uncut hair and other emblems). Even the slogans being chanted denoted the religion. Muslims shouted, *Allah hu Akbar* and *Nara e Takbeer* (God is the greatest); *Pakistan zindabad* (long live Pakistan); or *Hass ke lia hey Pakistan larr ke lengey Hindustan* (with a laugh we got Pakistan and will get whole of India by fight). Hindus chanted, *Bajrang Bali ki jay, Bharat mata ki jai* (a battle cry celebrating Hanuman, the Hindu monkey God that appears in the epic *Ramayan*). And Sikhs roared, *bole so nihal* (whoever utters shall be fulfilled) and *Raj kare ga khalsa* (pure Sikhs, or Khalsa, will rule). Clothing (burqas), hair, and other religious emblems also highlighted religious differences.

Unfortunately, even today we still live in a world of religious profiling. My family, for instance, has been feared simply because of our appearance. After 9/11, I was refused entry to a restaurant because I was wearing a turban. And my son was removed from a plane when other passengers objected to the way he looked. For us, air travel remains a fraught experience.

Because of religious profiling, hate crimes and the murder of innocent Sikhs and Muslims continue. In the United States, in the month following 9/11, Sikhs experienced more than 300 documented cases of violence and discrimination because their turban and beard led to mistaken religious profiling. Even in 2017—sixteen years after 9/11—a man was shot in Washington State. His crime? Being Sikh.

Discrimination, profiling, and hate crimes are as old as religion itself. During the time of Partition, religious profiling had mass catastrophic consequences.

I CONTEND THAT religion is the single most important environmental factor that fosters violence. When young children are exposure to fanatical teachings in their places of worship and religious schools and madrasas, it affects their worldview. This is how religious fanatics, zealots, and suicide bombers are created. Psychologist Susan Pinker sums it up like this: "Combine extreme religion's blinders with social ostracism, then season with the testosterone-driven aggressive impulses often found among disaffected young men and you can end up with a lethal stew."

From the first day we have been fighting the wrong enemy; our common enemy is religion, which dictates upon us division and partition.

—M. F. Moonzajer

The Role of Groups

Most violence has its roots in the cognitive construction of in-groups and out-groups. We typically divide people into two categories: *us* and *them*, a mental feat not exclusive to humans (Berreby; Cikara). *Us/them* divisions apply to race, ethnicity, income, gender, age, wage, and countless other splits. For instance, in India, a crowd sympathetic to Indira Gandhi (*us*) followed her funeral procession and later killed every Sikh (*them*) in sight, because Mrs. Gandhi was killed by her Sikh bodyguard. Most *us/them* distinctions are made subconsciously and are based on complex categories into which we instantly and unknowingly group other people. We consciously may only be aware that that we find comfort in in-groups, such as clans and religions.

The distinction between *us* and *them* is ancient and hardwired in us. Within fifty milliseconds, the brain processes the face of *them* differently from that of *us*. The image or presence of "thems"—people belonging to groups different than the ones with which we identify— stir up an ancient part of the brain: the amygdala. This brain region governs fear, anxiety and aggression. When activated, it can lead to violent outbursts and emotional explosions. These actions will be carried out unless another region of the brain called the orbitofrontal cortex can "put the brakes" on the amygdala. The orbitofrontal cortex can reflect on consequences of potentially violent impulses and stop the amygdala from acting irrationally (Raine; Miczek, Siever).

There's another part of the brain associated with facial recognition, the fusiform cortex. When an individual sees an *us*, there is activity in this region; but when a person sees a *them*, there is an absence of activity. Also, *thems* can trigger the insula, a part of the brain that deals with disgust. This feeling of revulsion is typically reserved for the senses, but it can also govern moral disgust.

Us and *them* divisions go beyond brain structure. Brain chemistry is also involved. Brain cells communicate through chemicals known as neurotransmitters (Siever). One such neurotransmitter, called oxytocin, prompts cooperation and trust among members of a group, but it has an opposite effect toward those outside the group. Another neurotransmitter, called serotonin, can help activate the "brakes" of the brain and reduce aggression. Those lacking in serotonin exhibit higher levels aggression. And, of course, testosterone facilitates aggression (Miczek; Yanowitch).

While individuals can certainly be violent on their own, this aggression may be amplified in a group, when individuals collectively

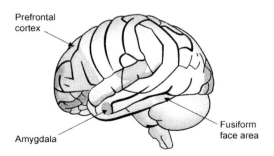

construct *us* and *them* distinctions. During Partition, most of the violence was committed by mobs rather than individuals. This fact makes it vital to understand the psychology and neurobiology of herd and mob mentality.

Groups will often engage in behavior contrary to personal moral standards: perfectly decent humans can be swept up in the power of the mob. Experiments—and history—have shown that individuals act more ruthlessly when in a group, and if the group is in competition with another group, even worse. Typically, people will act violent when one of three things happen:

○ They are able to reframe, justify, or rationalize their actions as being for the greater good.
○ They have anonymity, which can occur by being part of an in-group. Responsibility is spread among members of the group, so that no one individual will feel the weight of personal responsibility. Their actions are those of the group, the *us*.
○ Their moral standards are lowered.

Belonging to a group that is in competition with another group or that has targeted another group as its enemy can cause an individual to slowly or quickly satisfy all three criteria. Immoral actions are committed for the sake of the group. Action is justified in pursuit of goals, responsibility is spread among all members of the group, and the barriers of morality can be psychologically cracked.

The medial prefrontal cortex, or mPFC, is a brain region that carries out acts of self-reflection. It activates when a person thinks about his or her own personality, physicality, and morality, among other things. Likewise, it will also turn on when we hear someone else talking about us. When someone is engaging in malicious acts for the sake of a group, their mPFC will activate significantly *less*. When this happens, he or she is no longer an individual, but is now part of the group. While this deindividualization can lead to positive outcomes and communal acts of generosity, often the opposite is the case. When personal moral compasses have been sabotaged, the members of a mob do not reflect on their own actions.

Violence and Religion

Violence is as old as the universe and has been prevalent in most species. Hunter-gatherers used violence to protect their territory, families, and, in particular, women. As humans gathered into villages and, eventually, cities, many issues regarding territory and possessions were settled amicably. As people grouped together, the need arose for governance, and there appeared authorities such as kings and monarchs.

Many of these rulers assumed not only temporal but also spiritual authority, for instance, the Egyptians pharaohs. Most religions, however, worshipped divine gods. Oftentimes, these gods tempered violent tendencies in its worshippers. For instance, Romans dealt with adversities such as drought and sickness by seeking help from many gods and goddesses. Hindus have Shiva, Vishnu, Brahma, and others. To some degree, turning to gods and goddesses for relief helped resolve or avoid violence.

Later, the children of Abraham created Judaism, Christianity, and Islam, ushering in an era of unprecedented religious violence against one another. These religions also have conflict with offshoots or splinter sects within the religion. Among the three Abrahamic religions, Islam continues to be the most violent and in fact is getting worse. There was only a small period of some peace during the Ottoman Empire, when it began to consider Western ideas, which had some influence. Later in Islam, scripture was interpreted by mullahs to justify hatred for infidels. The mullahs glorify Shahidi sacrifice (martyrdom) for the religion with promises of a glamourous afterlife in heaven. These teachings have given birth to suicide bombings. The Middle East is mired in Shia-Sunni conflict, and the violence is being exported across the globe.

Intra-religious and interreligious conflict abounds in our current day: consider India (Kashmir), Sri Lanka (Tamil tigers), Yemen (Houthi insurgency) and Myanmar (Rohingya), to name a few. All these places of conflict have varying hues of religion, nationalism, populism, income inequality, ethnic cleansing, and the last vestiges of dictators. The main culprit is a lack of modernity.

WHEN I WAS a ten-year-old boy, I saw evidence of people acting without moral compasses. During Partition, most of the violence was committed by mobs rather than individuals. Perhaps that is why I have been on a quest throughout my adult life to understand the psychology and neurobiology of herd and mob mentality, and why I find the developments in these scientific disciplines to be so compelling and worthy of consideration.

Part 7

Seventy Years after Partition: My Thoughts

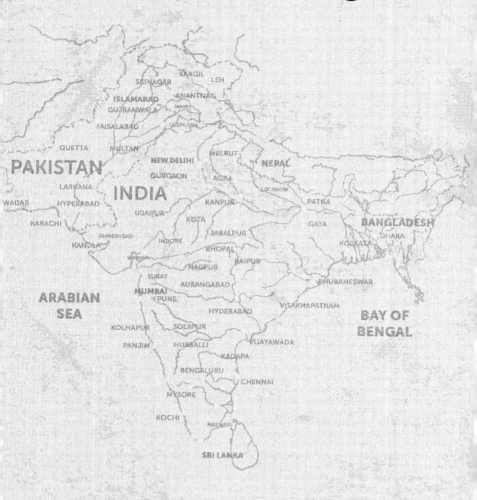

Love to Be Loved, Hate to Be Hated

L ove and hatred are basic traits of human character and determine our response to environments. While love and empathy are innate characteristics, observed in infants, hatred and aggression creep in later, as a Darwinian response to a survival challenge. This challenge could be physical existence or financial, political, territorial, or religious survival. All these played a role in the hatred that developed within communities. Religion was the conductor of this evil orchestra during the partition of Punjab. Mosques, Gurdwaras, and temples were the incubators. The religious communities harbored hatred because of perceived mistreatment, both historical and recent.

The history of Punjab has been marked by alternating periods of hatred and periods of peace. For instance, in the early sixteenth century, there was immense hatred during the Muslim invasion by the Mughal Baber. A classic Sikh poem has Guru Nanak confronting Baber: *pap the jang le kabulon dhia joru mange daan ve Lalo* (Baber came with a marriage party of evil and demanded a bride as a gift). Then, in the mid-sixteenth century, the Moghul emperor Akbar ruled over a time of peace. During the seventeenth century, there was a period of great resentment when the Mughal emperor Aurangzeb forced conversion to Islam. The Sikhs and their gurus were persecuted. A disciple of Guru Gobind Singh, Banda Bahadur created revengeful havoc against the Muslim community during this period. Later, during reign of the Sikh emperor Ranjit Singh, there was relative calm.

Then the British conquered Punjab and brought law and order but orchestrated religious boundaries, further splitting Punjabi society. Tensions between Muslims and Sikhs and Hindus were inflamed in 1920s Punjab by publication of the controversial book *Rangeela Rasul*, which offended the Muslim community because of its less-than-pious portrayal of the prophet Mohammed (Ahmed). The relationship between religious communities further deteriorated when the Muslim community claimed that during times of Maharaja Ranjit Singh, a mosque in Lahore had been demolished and Gurdwara Shaheed ganj constructed in its place. During these tense years, there was also talk about independence and British exit. When after World War II the British decided to leave in a hurry, confusion, chaos, and uncertainty reigned.

Punjabis leaned on their religions for protection and guidance. *Badmashis* (thugs), rogues, and opportunist politicians took advantages. Mosques, Gurdwaras, and temples were the only places for people to vent their feelings. Mullahs, Granthis, and Hindu priests felt they had failed in their responsibility if they did not raise their slogan: Religion in danger! While Sikh Granthis and the Hindu priests were kept in check by their respective communities, mullahs continued to preach violence against infidels, even in the West.

During this time:

Muslims were unhappy due to

- income disparity compared to Sikhs and Hindus
- Hindu moneylenders
- social boycott (devout Hindus did not allow Muslims in their kitchens and treated Muslims more like untouchables)
- humiliation (minority Sikhs had ruled them not long ago; also, the Muslim educated class felt crestfallen when the Ottoman Empire collapsed after World War I)

Hindus and Sikhs were unhappy due to

- foreign invaders (Muslims) now wanted part of India for themselves
- forced conversion by Muslims
- desecration of Hindu and Sikh shrines
- cruelty to Sikhs and Sikh gurus
- looting of property and abduction of women
- a sometimes tax on non-Muslims
- cow slaughter

Over and above these items, Muslims and Sikhs and Hindus had distinctly different ways of living, which I have outlined beginning on page 137. Jinnah had clearly stated that Muslims had nothing in common with Hindus.

Given this background, it is easy to imagine why India—Punjab and Bengal—had to be partitioned. The atmosphere became so poisoned when the British decided to leave that none of my grandfather's Muslim friends had the courage to console or counsel him during these times.

The current emotional interaction between Indian and Pakistani friends seems back to normal, as it was before Partition; however, each side remains guarded, treating the other as guests. Nobody is keen to return to live in their country of birth.

Religious reconciliation is still far off. The younger generation may not understand the emotional feelings of friendship the older generation had with those across the boundary line; to them it is all history. The younger generation mostly desires economic development and peace. Modernity is the hope.

It all reminds me of East and West Punjab: "Oh, East is East and West is West, and never the twain shall meet" (Rudyard Kipling).

....

Oh, East is East and West is West, and never the twain shall meet.

—Rudyard Kipling

....

Winners and Losers

At the time of Partition, Indian society was highly polarized on religious grounds. Even before Partition, Hindus and Sikhs had a deep-seated hatred for Muslims, and the opposite was true as well. Though there were instances of friendships between individuals of different religions—such as those between my grandfather and the Muslim hunchback potter and the Muslim Sher Mohammed—it was a rare thing. And even within these friendships, there was religious and cultural discrimination. For instance, a Muslim was not welcome in a Hindu kitchen, and a Hindu would not eat anything touched by a Muslim.

Because of the poison of religious bigotry and the environment of political upheaval, Partition was inevitable. The accompanying violence, however, could have been avoided. In my opinion, the main causes leading to violence were as follows:

- inexperienced leadership of all parties at the national level
- poor judgment on the part of Jinnah. The Muslim League became too powerful, and Jinnah could not put the genie back in bottle

even if he had wanted to. His ideas had resonated too powerfully with everyday Muslims, who demanded a separate country.

- hurry on the part of the British
- leaders on both sides using religion as the rallying instrument
- leaders being more interested in independence than its consequences

The prolonged period of uncertainty in the weeks before Partition gave militias on all sides—Sikh *jathas*, Muslim League guards, and Rashtriya Swayamsevak Sangh (RSS)—enough time to group. If all parties had been given more time to think and move slowly under British protection, violence might have been lessened.

FOR FAMILIES TOUCHED by Partition, it affected everything. The consequences of Partition did not end for my family and others by just crossing the border to India. For the next several years, my family moved from one place to another until settling in our final village, Nawan Pind Mehmowala. Our family—like most other Sikh refugees—had to develop relationships with new neighbors, civil servants, and local politicians and reestablish livelihoods. Despite those difficult days, I consider my family a winner in the long run. From an agrarian family living in Chattha Chak No. 46, we moved to India and eventually became urban elite with footprints abroad.

Other families also rose from the ashes of upheaval. Many refugees from Pakistan became famous writers, poets, and businessmen, including Khushwant Singh (writer), Amrita Pritam (poet laureate), Kuldip Nayar (journalist), the Kapur family (of Bollywood fame), and Om Prakash Munjal (businessman, Hero Cycles). Perhaps the most notable onetime refugee is Manmohan Singh, an economist who became prime minister of India from 2004 to 2014.

Countries were also winners and losers. Six and a half decades later, Pakistan and India have taken separate paths. For most of India, it was a victory lap, while Punjab, Bengal, Kashmir, and the princely states were losers. But the biggest loser, in my opinion, was Pakistan.

With Partition, Jinnah got less than he wanted. Owing to geographical and logistical reasons, Pakistan could not remain within India; it could exist only in the periphery of India—Punjab and Bengal. He could not claim the whole of Punjab because the Sikhs and Hindus outnumbered Muslims in east Punjab. Furthermore, Bengal was miles away from west Punjab, and there were cultural and linguistic differences between the two; hence they had only real estate value. Jinnah himself regretted that he got a "maimed, mutilated and moth-eaten Pakistan." After a honeymoon period between East Pakistan and West Pakistan, East Pakistan declared independence from Pakistan, becoming Bangladesh in 1971. Ever since Partition, a smaller Pakistan has lived with the constant threat from its bigger neighbor.

Jinnah was a powerful dictatorial leader, but he failed to groom further leadership. In the period of political uncertainty after his death, army generals took over, and the politics of populism propelled Pakistan further into an Islamic state. Today, religious cleansing continues, and non-Muslims as well as Muslims at the fringes of pure Islam are under attack. Non-state actors, with the blessing of the army, flourish in Pakistan and neighboring Afghanistan and conduct terrorist attacks in Kashmir and other parts of India. The same organizations are now a threat to Pakistan.

Did Jinnah do the right thing for the wrong cause or the wrong thing for the right cause? He wanted freedom for Muslims, but because of his leadership, Muslims are now a minority in India; thus, he did not fulfill the very purpose of his ambitions for Muslims.

Pakistan became an Islamic republic, where religion and politics are intertwined. A few periods of democracy were interrupted by military dictators. The small minorities of non-Muslims, such as Christians, Hindus, and Sikhs, are second-rate citizens, and even offshoots of Islam, such as Ahmadis, are subjected to violence. Shias are discriminated against by majority Sunnis. Pakistan's claim to Kashmir has resulted in skirmishes and wars with India and has sapped Pakistan's resources, hindering its development.

Pakistan's periodic military rule may not be relevant to Partition, but it is partially responsible for continued animosity with its nuclear neighbor, India. This situation was addressed by Christophe Jaffrelot in his recent book *Pakistan at the Crossroads*, which quotes the views of other authors including Aqil Shah and Mohammad Waseem. Jaffrelot suggests that the Pakistan army, to stay in power, continually foments anti-India feelings and permanent fear—almost a phobia of India—in Pakistan. The army also encourages non-state actors to commit cross-border terrorism. (Meanwhile, Pakistan's neighbors to the west are spreading religious fanaticism. Shias and Sunnis are constantly battling, and minorities there are under fire.) All these things have given rise to the Pakistan Taliban, which conducts terrorism in its own country. All this is detrimental to the Pakistani society.

Violence continues in the Middle East. It appears violence has been part of Islam from its very beginning, in the seventh century. After all, Mohammed built an army as he was establishing Islam. Could the violence be environmental/geographical or religious? Maybe it is both. Regardless, the violence has had an impact on the rest of the world. One sad side of this violent behavior has been the recent large-scale destruction of icons of the Roman civilization (such as the monuments in Palmyra, Syria) and the Buddhist civilizations (including the Buddhas of Bamiyan, Afghanistan), as well as several centuries of mass forced conversions in India. This violent behavior is embedded deep and will take a long time to change. Surely education for all and the empowerment of women will make a difference.

India, meanwhile, has moved in a different direction from Pakistan. The British never thought a poor, illiterate, heterogeneous country could have democracy; but despite a heterogeneous culture, India has nascent democracy and secularism. Religious political parties were gradually marginalized. (If futurists are correct, religion will not be a rallying force in years to come.) Credit goes to India's people, leaders, and army.

India continues to lunge along, trying its best to provide safeguards to minorities. Efforts to carve out Khalistan in the north and dissident movements in the east have eased. With time, I believe India will also discard Hindu nationalism. (Multicultural and multi-religious democracies such as America and Canada are the guiding light of future.) The separation of religion and the state bodes well, and I hope Pakistan will gradually move in that direction.

In my opinion, Partition was ultimately a good decision for India. A united India would have been in constant chaos. I agree with the writer Aakar Patel, who suggests that undivided India would have been a poorer country. Religious conflict would have consumed its resources. Even Nehru said, "Division is better than a union of unwilling parts." Jinnah himself said to a British interviewer, "We are different beings. . . . There is nothing in life that links us [Hindus and Muslims] together."

It is difficult to imagine the two religions could ever agree. An undivided India would have been a dictatorial military regime no different from the Raj. India took advantage of democracy, while Pakistan suffered from military rule and did not nurture a secular and pluralistic society. I hope in time Pakistan will have democracy for the good of its people as well as its neighbors.

Freedom does not come easy. There is always a price to pay. The rest of India should be thankful to Punjab and Bengal for paying the major share of this price.

God bless all those who suffered so that we could all enjoy freedom.

Muslim League wins; Muslims lose.

Social and Political Changes

During the past seventy years, there has been continual change in the world, including the spread of democracies, urbanization, strides in human longevity, reduction of poverty, reduced birth rates in advanced societies, and, unfortunately, increasing income disparity.

Punjab during this period, has experienced special social and political events because of Partition. For example, the princely states were integrated in India, and later their privy purses were discontinued. Gradually, the princes became poorer and the politicians became richer. The big farmers got hit when maximum acreage, which was previously unlimited, was reduced to fifteen acres per farmer. Banks and many other enterprises were nationalized to the detriment of the economy. A free market was sacrificed for political gains, as the state took over many enterprises, giving more power to the politicians. The old generation of leaders who fought for freedom and went to jail have been replaced by politicians who want to be elected to become rich and be reelected to hold on to their ill-gotten wealth. This is also the view of the election commissioner of India.

I LEFT MY ancestral land fifty years ago and now view Punjabi society from the distance of time and geography. Migrants to the West, like me, often view our motherland unfavorably. With this in mind, I do have some personal observations about some of the systemic problems in modern-day India:

o Farmers near big cities are becoming richer due to the appreciated price of land, while others with less land holdings are getting poorer. Land owned by families is being further subdivided among siblings. Farmers are not being educated about other possible livelihoods. For many, *jaddy* (inherited) land has become a liability.

o Society is less caring and compassionate. Fewer people stop to help those lying injured on the roadside. Many onlookers do not want to deal with a visit to the police station. Indians in general shun civil responsibility.

o Weddings are getting more lavish and last many days. To do so is morally unbecoming of a society with so many poor who cannot afford three meals a day.

o The charitable land of Gurus, mahatmas, and Bhagat Puran Singh has gone amiss. We have lost the moral requirement of charitable giving. Before Partition, Sir Ganga Ram in west Punjab was the most charitable human being. Now, in spite of riches, we have not created the likes of him in seventy years in east Punjab.

A brief Partition-related episode I heard may be of interest to readers: At the height of religious frenzy at Lahore during Partition, a mob climbed the statue of Sir Ganga Ram and painted the face black. They put a garland of torn shoes around the statue. (In Punjab of those days, this was a revengeful act of disrespect, in this case to a Hindu considered an enemy.) During this ill-conceived adventure, one climber fell and broke his arm. Guess where they took him for treatment? Ganga Ram Hospital (Ahmed).

Late in 2016, I was in the office of Thomas Tayeri, MD, in Palo Alto, California, for my wife's eye exam. On the video screen, I saw Dr. Tayeri traveling to various places in poor countries to restore vision to many. His charity took him to Jodhpur in Rajasthan, India. When I saw that, I thought, "We in India are not short of eye doctors but of a strong sense of charity and giving." Foreign charities fill the void. At cocktail parties, we praise their work and commitment for the good of humankind but stop short of doing good works ourselves.

- Travel agents are making false promises of visas abroad to poor Punjabis seeking opportunity overseas. To prey on uneducated or desperate people is just wrong, perhaps corrupt.
- At this moment, the democracy of Punjab is of the corrupt, by the corrupt, and for many corrupt. The poor, the illiterate, and the few honest people are being disenfranchised with promises of liquor, cash, and false promises of jobs.
- This frustration leads to addiction—a big problem in Punjab. Corrupt leaders may benefit from the gangs and drug cartels.

Sad as it is, going to jail for a crime is no longer a stigma socially or politically. Perhaps public shaming should be reinstituted. How about putting the prisoner on a donkey with a garland of shoes hung around his neck with his face colored black? This type of shaming worked in the past in Punjab and has been practiced in Pakistan in the not-distant past. It is certainly better than more permanent and violent forms of punishment, such as blinding repeat offenders in central India or, according to the *Tribune India*, tattooing *jeb katri* (pickpocket) on the forehead of a few women in that trade in Punjab (the police officers who did this went to jail). Also, not long ago, a law in the Middle East allowed the amputation of certain body parts as punishment for crimes, especially for thieves and sex offenders. This is all to bring shame to the shameless when civilized punishments lose their intended effect.

Civil liberty organizations in India have no defense when a large majority of parliamentarians have criminal records. In jail, the politicians are provided all the luxury. One important prisoner even was found having breakfast with his jailor.

Punjab is burning again.

Many years ago, according to author Hardev Singh Virk, Professor Puran Singh said about democracy and the new leaders of Punjab, "the giants are gone and now tiny dwarfs flutter and shake their wings" and "unless the change be wrought within, the volcanoes will burst."

The situation is probably no different in west Punjab. The issue of corruption was foremost in people's mind when Malcolm Darling interviewed villagers on his journey through Punjab in 1946.

It is time for change, which must come from within Punjabis.

Laggi nazar punjab nu
Audi nazar utaro.
Le ke mirchan kaurrian.
Aede. sir ton waro
(Punjab has been seized upon by evil spirits and cure [voodoo] this by waving bitter chilies on its head)

—Surjit Patar

Laggi Nazr punjab nu
SURJIT PAATAR (1945–)

PUNJABI

Paatar did not write this poem about Partition; instead, its subject is another tragic event in Punjab's history. Nonetheless, it is relevant to the tragedy of Partition. The poem describes violence, as well as fallen turbans, a sign of dishonor among Sikhs. Paatar suggests that evil spirits have overtaken Punjab and that the remedy should be pouring burning red chilies over the heads of the victims and the diseased (a medieval Punjabi remedy). At this time, there is no English translation.

ਲੱਗੀ ਨਜ਼ਰ ਪੰਜਾਬ ਨੂੰ

ਲੱਗੀ ਨਜ਼ਰ ਪੰਜਾਬ ਨੂੰ, ਏਦ੍ਹੀ ਨਜ਼ਰ ਉਤਾਰੋ।
ਲੈ ਕੇ ਮਰਿਚਾਂ ਕੌੜੀਆ, ਏਹਦੇ ਸਿਰ ਤੋ ਵਾਰੇ
ਸਿਰ ਤੋ ਵਾਰੇ, ਵਾਰ ਕੇ, ਅੱਗ ਦੇ ਵਿਚ ਸਾੜੇ
ਲੱਗੀ ਨਜ਼ਰ ਪੰਜਾਬ ਨੂੰ, ਏਦ੍ਹੀ ਨਜ਼ਰ ਉਤਾਰੋ।

ਮਰਿਚਾਂ ਜਹਰਿ ਕੌੜੀਆਂ, ਮਰਿਚਾਂ ਸਿਰ ਸੜੀਆਂ
ਕਧਿਰੋ ਲੈਣ ਨਾ ਜਾਣੀਆਂ, ਵਹਿੜੇ ਵਿਚ ਬੜੀਆਂ
ਪਹਿਲੀ ਭਰਵੀ ਫਸਲ, ਇਨਾਂ ਦੀ ਓਦੋ ਲੱਗੀ
ਜਦ ਆਪੇ ਪੰਜਾਬੀਆਂ, ਪੰਜਾਬੀ ਛੱਡੀ

ਤੇ ਫਿਰ ਅਗਲੀ ਫਸਲ ਦੇ, ਬੀ ਗਏ ਖਲਿਰੇ
ਵੱਢੇ ਗਏ ਨਰਿਦੇਸ਼ ਜਦੋ, ਰਾਹ ਜਾਂਦੇ ਮਾਰੇ
ਵੱਢਣ ਵਾਲੇ ਕੌਣ ਸਨ ਇਹ ਭੇਤ ਨਾ ਲੱਗਾ
ਪਰ ਬੇਦੋਸਾ ਖੂਨ ਤਾਂ ਪੱਗਾਂ ਸਿਰ ਲੱਗਾ

ਉਹੀ ਛੱਟੇ ਖੂਨ ਦੇ, ਬਣ ਗਏ ਬਹਾਨਾ
ਸਾਡੀ ਪੱਗ ਨੂੰ ਪੈ ਗਿਆ ਆਪਣਾ ਬੇਗਾਨਾ
ਜਿੱਥੇ ਤਕ ਛਾਂ ਤਖਤ ਦੀ ਅੱਗਾਂ ਹੀ ਅੱਗਾਂ
ਚੌਂਕ-ਚੁਰਾਹੇ ਸੜਦੀਆਂ ਪੱਗਾਂ ਹੀ ਪੱਗਾਂ

ਪੱਤੇ ਬੂਟੇ ਡੋਡੀਆਂ ਫੁੱਲਾਂ ਦੀਆਂ ਲੜੀਆਂ
ਸਭ ਕੁਝ ਅੱਗ ਵਿਚ ਸੜ ਗਿਆ
ਮਰਿਚਾਂ ਨਾ ਸੜੀਆਂ
ਉਹ ਮਰਿਚਾਂ ਜ਼ਹਿਰੀਲੀਆਂ
ਏਹਦੇ ਸਿਰ ਤੋਂ ਵਾਰੇ
ਸਿਰ ਤੋਂ ਵਾਰੇ ਵਾਰ ਕੇ
ਅੱਗ ਦੇ ਵਿਚ ਸਾੜੇ ।

ਅੱਗ ਪਤਿਰਾਂ ਦੀ ਜੀਭ ਹੈ
ਉਦੀ ਭੇਟਾ ਚਾੜ੍ਹੇ
ਉਹ ਪਤਿਰਾਂ ਦਾ ਬੀਜਿਆ
ਬੀਤੇ ਸੰਗ ਸਾੜੇ ।

ਲੱਗੀ ਨਜ਼ਰ ਪੰਜਾਬ ਨੂੰ, ਏਹਦੀ ਨਜ਼ਰ ਉਤਾਰੇ।
ਲੈ ਕੇ ਮਰਿਚਾਂ ਕੌੜੀਆਂ ਏਹਦੇ ਸਿਰ ਤੋਂ ਵਾਰੇ।

ਸੁਰਜੀਤ ਪਾਤਰ

Modernity and Violence

While Punjab since Partition has struggled with challenges both common and unique, it has made many strides. Some of these can be attributed to an embrace of modernity.

"Modernity" is a term with which many readers may not be familiar. Modernity refers to both a period in history (the modern era) *and* its accompanying norms and attitudes, and scientific and technological advances.

Modernity can help advance and strengthen societies. Most Western cultures are examples of modernity at work. Western cultures, for instance, lead in technology, science, higher education, mass literacy, standards of living, and functional democracy—all hallmarks of modernity. This isn't to say that modernity is all positive. As with any philosophy or phenomenon, there are negatives associated with it, including the development of weapons of mass destruction, the erosion of unique local cultures and traditions, and environmental damage caused by industrial development.

In the East, Turkey is an example of a country that tried to move its society toward modernity during the twentieth century. According to writer Albert Hourani, the Ottoman Empire at its height began embracing modernity much as Western societies had. In the nineteenth century, Ottoman, Egyptian, and Tunisian rulers sent their scholars to France to study the Enlightenment and other philosophies of modernity. These scholars returned home and implemented changes in scientific and legal thought, as well as other reforms, which, in many cases, were antithetical to conservative Islamic thought. After the fall of the Ottoman Empire at the end of World War I, however, many Muslim-majority cultures began shifting away from modernity. The materialistic values of the West—along with some Western nations' continued colonization of other countries—did not mesh with Islamic values. Unfortunately, modern Turkey has now embraced a more conservative view and is moving toward political Islam.

Other countries have overtly rejected modernity and have instead used oil industry profits to promote conservative Islamic thought. For instance, the House of Saud has funded the spread of Salafism, an ultraconservative interpretation of Islam.

From my point of view, this trend is a mistake. For only modernity will provide the tools—scientific, technological, social, and governmental—to solve the world's pressing problems. It may take years to bear fruit, but modernity is good for all of us as evidenced by the increased longevity, affluence, means of communication, improved infrastructure, and reduction in poverty experienced by Western cultures. Other benefits include stronger democracy, separation of religion and state, secularism, stronger rule of law, property rights, and the care of the poor and disabled. Modernity creates peaceful and less violent societies.

While modernity can propel countries forward, it can also positively affect individuals. For instance, modernity values education for all, the empowerment of women (and a rejection of polygamy), and reforms in Sharia law. All three of these values were demonstrated in an August 2017 verdict by the Indian Supreme Court that ruled triple *talaq* (instant divorce) unconstitutional and illegal. Before this ruling, a Muslim man simply had to utter the word "talaq" three times to divorce his wife—a practice that sustained patriarchy. With this ruling, India has joined other nations with large Muslim populations that have outlawed this practice, including Pakistan, Bangladesh, Iran, Egypt, Iraq, Sudan, Egypt, and Iran, among others.

Greater education can also help an individual function in the global world. Knowledge of international languages, dress, manners, and norms are important to function in global world. I once had a doctor visit me from south India who had little knowledge of other countries. While we were dining together, he began eating the rice and curry with his hand, the curry dripping down to his elbow. But he was smart and observant, and he quickly switched to cutlery when he saw others using cutlery. Education is the great equalizer in a society and a step on the path of meritocracy. Achievement and ability should prevail over prejudice, color, cast, creed and nationality.

ISLAMIC COUNTRIES SEEM especially resistant to modernity. Perhaps this is one cause of the persistent nature of the violence emanating from Islamic countries. To me, the rest of the world, other than the Islamic countries, seems open to modernity.

I'd like to highlight three examples from my life that make me hopeful that young people in Islamic countries will begin to reject the fundamentalism of their countries.

- o A few years ago, my daughter worked with a young female Muslim physician-in-training from Karachi, Pakistan. The young woman's family arranged her marriage to a less educated man from her same tribe. The marriage was an unhappy one, so she asked for a divorce, against her parents' wishes. After the divorce, she married a non-Muslim and is now happily married and the mother of two children.

o I have an acquaintance in the United States who is a highly educated university professor whose family lives in Lahore. Against his parents' wishes, he married a beautiful and accomplished Catholic professional. The marriage was arranged by a Sikh colleague, and his family did not participate in the wedding. He is happy and prospering in his profession and in his marriage.

o In September 2016, twenty students from Pakistan visited Chandigarh, the capital city of Punjab, to attend the eleventh annual Global Youth Peace festival. At the event, they enjoyed Punjabi hospitality. Unfortunately, as this event was taking place, there was a resurgence of hostilities at the Indo-Pak border, around the town of Uri. The Pakistani students' parents called for them to come home, but the students refused to cut their visit short. The students commented that the *people* of Pakistan want to improve their relationship with India and blamed *politicians* for creating tension between the two countries.

I interpret these three examples as moves toward modernity. I praise young people for their courage to challenge centuries-old traditions and adopt the good values of the modernity of the West.

I am still, however, reminded that repressive traditions continue to hold sway in many Islamic countries. For example, a few years ago, an Egyptian physician friend showed me old photographs of girls on a beach in Egypt wearing bikinis. Given the current political climate in Egypt, such a thing is no longer possible. Also, a few months ago, a young girl in Pakistan was killed by her own brother because she was too active on social media and had taken a picture with a mullah. This represents *modernity being sacrificed on the altar of religion.*

The move toward modernity will not be quick or easy. As with any change, there is always peer pressure to maintain the old ways.

I experienced this when I joined a rural college in Punjab in 1953. Anyone wearing trousers or a suit or who spoke English was ridiculed as an English Sahib. Part of this mockery was a reaction to British colonialism, and part was a reaction to modernity as a social change. Still today, in India, many politicians abstain from wearing Western dress when they're in India, thinking they will garner more votes; however, they wear Western clothes on their foreign visits.

In Pakistan, peer pressure and religious edicts result in far-reaching restraints on freedom of thought and choice of dress and food, and even the person you marry. When individual Pakistanis rebel against this pressure, they face consequences. Some resort to subterfuge. For instance, some of my Muslim friends drink alcohol behind locked doors; others mix it with coke to disguise it. I am reminded of a flight I took from Dubai to New York on which two women boarded wearing burqas. A few minutes after the flight took off, the women went to the plane's rest rooms and came out dressed in skirts—and no burqas. They loved Western dress but lacked the courage to dress as they chose in their own country. During the flight, it dawned on me that I was the only one left wearing a religious symbol—a turban. In some ways, my turban is no different from their burqas, which they had the courage to discard. A Sikh turban is a religious symbol of Sikhism but a handicap to job opportunities in the United States. Further, wearing a turban encourages religious profiling and hate crimes. What would my grandfather's reaction be now to the saying "When in Rome, do as the Romans do"? Back when I was a boy telling my grandfather about this idiom, he was not contemplating modernity and globalization. And later, when he crossed the Indo-Pak border, modernity was the last thing on his mind. He was thinking more like a hunter-gatherer, looking for food and shelter on the other side. If he were alive today, perhaps he would think differently about the world; perhaps he would see the value of knowing the norms of other countries.

All symbols and rituals of religion and culture are hindrances to modernity and work against the welfare of the state in the long run. The march of modernity will destroy these ill-conceived walls.

Violence has many causes. We have to find as many cures. Modernity and religious fundamentalism are dueling forces, and in time, modernity will win and fundamentalism will lose.

Hindu and Muslim Fundamentalists

While the wounds of Partition are healing, the Bharatiya Janata Party (BJP) and RSS in India continue their anti-Pakistan and anti-Muslim propaganda. For example, in 1992, the sixteenth-century Babri Mosque in Ayodhya was demolished by rioting Hindus after a political rally, and in 2002, there were days of anti-Muslim riots in Gujarat. Some fundamentalist organizations in Pakistan continue to attack across the border, including attacks on the Indian parliament in 2001 and the Taj Hotel in Mumbai in 2008.

The Middle East is embroiled in a Shia-Sunni conflict with spillover into neighboring countries. The Islamic State appeared on the scene in 2003 and began a campaign of violence against religions at the fringe of Islam, such as the Ahmadis, Zoroastrians, Baha'is, and Zubaids. Christians and Jews are targets as well.

If history is any guide, in spite of all this, peace will prevail. For example, after many centuries of wars in Europe, most of Europe is now more politically and economically connected through the European Union than ever before. Germany and Japan and the United States are now close friends and allies. Distant is the memory of World War

II. This pattern has occurred in other parts of the world with other former enemies. Both India and Pakistan should improve their relationship and encourage mutual trade and tourism. They should worry less about each other and more about the dragon in the north: China.

Educated, progressive citizens of both countries must speak up for peace and reject the path of fundamentalism. A silent majority cannot wait and watch; they have a responsibility to guide the youth.

Religious Reconciliation

Efforts at religious reconciliation have been made periodically since the time Muslims conquered India. Sometimes the push for unity came from a conquering force, sometimes from the writings of mystic poets-saints, sometimes from religious leaders, academics, or social leaders, and occasionally from political leaders. For instance, the sixteenth-century Mughal emperor Akbar took steps to bring the two religions closer by marrying a Hindu, Rajput princess. He also attempted to promote a new religion, Dīn-I *Ilāhī*, probably a compromise between Hinduism and Islam. His descendent, Prince Dara Shikoh, translated the sacred Hindu book, the Bhagavad Gita, into Persian.

A relatively secular Sufi Muslim movement integrated the teaching of other religions into its teachings, which helped to bridge differences between the them. The early seventeenth-century Punjabi Sufi poet Bulleh Shah said, *Gal samajh laee te raolaa keeh Raam Raheem te Maula keeh.* (God is same with different names. If we understand this there is no confusion.) He went further, saying, *Masjid dha day,mander dha day ,dha day jo kuch dhenda, par bandey da dil na dhawein rub dillan wich rehnda.* (Demolish the mosque and Hindu temple, demolish everything in sight, but do not demolish the human heart because that is where god resides.) Many non-Muslims paid homage at Sufi shrines and *darghas* (shrines at graves of Muslim holy men). The Bhakti movement, a medieval Hindu movement that influenced Sikhism, emphasized unity and oneness. Writings of the fifteenth-century Sufi saint Bhagat Kabir—revered by Hindus, Muslims, and Sikhs—are found in Guru Granth Sahib and include, "*Awwal Allah Noor upaya, Kudrat ke sab Bande Ek Noor te sab jag upja kaun bhale, kaun mande.*" (God is above all. He sowed the seeds of humanity, and from that same seed grew all of humanity. All human beings are equal; nobody is good or bad.)

By the early nineteenth-century, Punjab was very secular. For instance, during the reign of the Sikh emperor Maharaja Ranjit Singh, Sikhs, Muslims, and Hindus fought side by side at the Battle of Sobraon, in 1846, against the British. Before World War II, the Muslim poet Iqbal wrote "*Mazhab nahin sikhata aapas mein bher rakhna*" (religion does not promote hatred and animosity). In the same era, Professor Puran Singh wrote, "*Punjab na Hindu. Na Muselman Punjab sara jeenda Guru de nam*") (Punjab is not Hindu or Muslman. It lives with the will of Guru.) One of Gandhi's favorite songs, "Ishwar, Allah Tere Nam" (Ishwar and Allah are God's name), emphasized unity.

In my own life, I saw examples of religious blending. My grandfather, a Sikh, was a devotee of a Muslim *faqir* (holy man). Each year, my grandfather would give an offering of a horse to demonstrate his devotion. Likewise, the journalist Kuldip Nayar's family, all Hindus, worshipped at the *dargha* of a holy Muslim *faqir* in their backyard. These *faqirs* were secular—not fanatics—and had a universal following, with Muslims, Sikhs, and Hindus devotees.

The last moment for religious reconciliation appeared before the independence movement, when all citizens, irrespective of religion, banded together against the Raj. However, the unity was temporary, and communal hatred reached an all-time high when independence was assured. Even the poet Iqbal changed his mind. He said "*China, Arab, hamara, Hindustan hamara. Muslim hain hum watan hein sara Jahan hamara.*" (China, Arab, and Hindustan are ours; we are Muslims and whole world is ours.) In 1927, Shaheed Bhagat Singh, a young Indian revolutionary, wrote the essay "Communal problem and its solutions," which includes this statement, "At present India is in a deplorable state. The adherents of one religion are sworn enemies of another faith." According to him, the press should have played an educated role and fostered love, but instead it chose to preach ignorance, narrowmindedness, and communalism to destroy our common heritage and nationalism (Karthik). Nehru later lamented the evils of religion, stating, "No country or people who are slaves to dogma and dogmatic mentality can progress."

Religious cleansing appeared with Partition, and a hateful attitude still prevails. Fanatic religious groups and cross-border terrorism still persist. A mindset of tit for tat between nuclear neighbors is dangerous. All this is due to a lack of modernity in illiterate, poor, and slave countries. Those who took part in this mayhem with the promises of reward in the afterlife of heaven and Jannat most likely will be betrayed.

Maybe Punjab did not need the Indian National Congress, Akali Dal, or the Muslim League; and perhaps it did not need Gandhi,

....

Masjid Dha de. Mandar dha de. Dha dey jo kush dhenda Per bande da dil na dhaweine, Rab dillan which renda. (Demolish the mosque and Hindu temple, demolish everything in sight, but do not demolish the human heart because that is where God resides.)

—Bulleh Shah
....

Nehru, or Jinnah. What it needed instead was holy men of various religions preaching unity, devotion, and love for all, but in secular terms—men such as Baba Nanak, Mian Mir, Bulleh Shah, and Sheikh Farid. Perhaps if their teachings had touched the hearts of all Punjabis, the people would have been spared decades of anguish and years of continued hatred in the name of religion.

Anthem of the People of India
MUHAMMAD IQBAL (1877–1938)

HINDI

A patriotic song originally composed in Urdu in 1904, this poem/lyric became popular as an anthem opposing British rule.

सारे जहां से अच्छा, हिन्दोस्तां हमारा
हम बुलबुलें हैं इसकी, यह गुलसितां हमारा

गुरबत में हों अगर हम, रहता है दिल वतन में
समझो वहीं हमें भी, दिल हो जहां हमारा

पर्वत वो सबसे ऊंचा, हमसाया आसमां का
वो संतरी हमारा, वो पासवां हमारा

गोदी में खेलती हैं, जिसकी हजरों नदियां
गुलशन है जिसके दम से, रश्के–जिनां हमारा

ऐ आबे–रौंदे–गंगा, वो दिन है याद तुझको
उतरा तेरे किनारे जब कारवां हमारा

मजहब नहीं सिखाता, आपस में बैर रखना
हिंदी हैं हम, वतन है, हिन्दोस्तां हमारा

यूनान, मिस्र, रोमा, सब मिट गए जहां से
अब तक मगर है बाकी, नामों निशां हमारा

कुछ बात है कि हस्ती, मिटती नहीं हमारी
सदियों रहा है दुश्मन, दौरे जहां हमारा

हकबाल कोई मरहूम, अपना नहीं जहां में
मालूम क्या किसी को दर्दे निहां हमारा

URDU

سارے جہاں سے اچھا ہندوستاں ہمارا
ہم بلبلیں ہیں اس کی، یہ گلستاں ہمارا
غربت میں ہوں اگر ہم، رہتا ہے دل وطن میں
سمجھو وہیں ہمیں بھی دل ہو جہاں ہمارا
پربت وہ سب سے اونچا، ہمسایہ آسماں کا
وہ سنتری ہمارا، وہ پاسباں ہمارا
گودی میں کھیلتی ہیں اس کی ہزاروں ندیاں
گلشن ہے جن کے دم سے رشکِ جناں ہمارا
اے آبِ رودِ گنگا! وہ دن ہیں یاد تجھ کو؟
اترا ترے کنارے جب کارواں ہمارا
مذہب نہیں سکھاتا آپس میں بیر رکھنا
ہندی ہیں ہم، وطن ہے ہندوستاں ہمارا
یونان و مصر و روما سب مٹ گئے جہاں سے

اب تک مگر ہے باقی نام و نشاں ہمارا
کچھ بات ہے کہ ہستی مٹتی نہیں ہماری
صدیوں رہا ہے دشمن دورِ زماں ہمارا
اقبال! کوئی محرم اپنا نہیں جہاں میں
معلوم کیا کسی کو دردِ نہاں ہمارا!

ENGLISH

Better than the entire world, is our Hindustan,
We are its nightingales, and it (is) our garden abode
If we are in an alien place, the heart remains in the
    homeland,
Know us to be nly there where our heart is.
Total tallest mountain, that shade-sharer of the sky,
It (is) our sentry, it (is) our watchman
In its lap where frolic thousands of rivers,
Whose vitality makes our garden the envy of Paradise.
O the flowing waters of the Ganges, do you remember that
    day
When our caravan first disembarked on your waterfront?
Religion does not teach us to bear animosity among
    ourselves
We are of Hind, our homeland is Hindustan.
In a world in which ancient Greece, Egypt, and Rome have
    all vanished without trace
Our own attributes (name and sign) live on today.
There is something about our existence for it doesn't get
    wiped

Even though, for centuries, the time-cycle of the world has
    been our enemy.
Iqbal! We have no confidant in this world
What does any one know of our hidden pain?

Darwin's Evolution:
Religious, Social, and Political

When Darwin wrote about evolution, he meant the evolution of living things. He emphasized survival of the fittest and the need for adaptation. He did not talk about social, political and religious evolution. But as with species, societies can survive only if they evolve and adapt to the needs of time and progress.

While the evolution of species takes millions of years, social, political and religious evolution can occur within cultures rather quickly. Societies that do not evolve for the good of citizens are left behind. Social and political evolution are easy, while religious change is challenging.

Hurrah for atheism, pantheism, and liberal humanism. They do not have to deal with religious bindings.

Religious faiths, meanwhile, are evolving in their own ways. Hinduism, for instance, has been changing over the centuries. For instance, in the nineteenth and twentieth centuries, new movements have modernized Hinduism, most importantly in Punjab, Arya Samaj. Sikhism, particularly in the West, has grudgingly accepted the shaving of hair and lack of *kirpan* (sword). Christianity has gone through reformations through the centuries and is evolving and struggling even today. The Catholic Church, for example, has experienced schisms, and debates continue over the celibacy of priests, gay marriage, birth control, homosexuality, and premarital sex. Other religions face other challenges. Judaism and Zoroastrianism are facing pressure in temple attendance. Buddhism has the virtue of nonviolence but is vulnerable to subjugation by others; in other words, it lacks Darwinian survival of the fittest. Jainism is the same.

Currently, Islam is resisting any change. Fatwas are served to those who challenge the tenants of Islam. (Salman Rushdie and Aayan Hirsi Ali are two recent examples known in the West.)

While Darwinian evolution marches onward, nonreversible and heedless of human desire, the same cannot be said for religious, social, and political evolution. These *are* reversible: social evolution in some societies has backslid or reversed course, to the detriment of these cultures and religions. If futurists are correct, during this century religion will be under siege. There is sound reasoning for their prophecy. Truthfulness, empathy and charity, and spirituality existed before organized modern religion was born. But some faith systems have been forced onto certain populations by colonization and monarchy. India, for example, was conquered by Muslims several centuries ago and later colonized by the British.

This cultural and religious mindset will be difficult to reverse, but societies may adapt to be less fanatical and more secular. Doing so will allow them to be part of the global conversation.

In the modern world, religion will not need muscle power; rather, it will need the power of spirituality and virtues. Societal evolution is first step to modernity.

Time as a Healer

With time, animosities among nations will dissipate. The enemies of great wars are friends now. Some formerly warring religions have learned to live together in peace, such as Catholics and Protestants in Northern Ireland. Shias and Sunnis will one day do the same, and other religions will follow. Nuclear neighbors, such as India and Pakistan, will move toward better relations, pushed or pulled there by factors such as public opinion, the army, political Islam, and Hindu nationalist BJP. Importantly, public opinion is most favorable to better relations at this moment. Mutual travel, trade, the exchange of performers and musicians, visiting scholars, and visitors to religious shrines will further cement the cracks of history and religion.

Such changes take a long time. The older generation of political leaders are gone. While some believe that with the demise of the generation—that is, the generation with emotional ties to the other country and friends of the other religion—hatred and animosity will increase. But I believe in modernity. I believe the younger generation will desire peace, economic development, and the well-being of their society. There will be less hunger for hegemony and territorial gains.

Perhaps, as writer Steve Coll suggests, India and Pakistan will find solutions working through backchannels.

I hope religions will take a back seat, lessening the influence of fanatic organizations and terrorism. Let it be that "the old order changeth, yielding place to new" (Alfred Tennyson).

Humankind and New Challenges

Mankind has made tremendous progress since its beginning as a society of cavemen and hunter-gatherers. Only a few years ago, modern breakthroughs in medicine, industrialization, the Internet, and space travel were only futurists' dreams.

Hunter-gatherers had conflicts with other groups for many reasons. Religion probably was not the main culprit. Sometime around the Roman period, religion became the temporal and spiritual authority, and from that time on, religion was a cause of conflict. Nationalism and ethnic and territorial ambitions were other reasons for conflict.

Industrialization made human beings more vulnerable to weapons of mass destruction. Also, bad actors and rogue states are a constant threat to civilizations and humankind. Communism as a threat has been replaced by religious zealotry, which is fueled when countries fail to integrate minority groups and immigrants into the mainstream.

These social issues need urgent attention. It is disheartening to know that most kings and dictators are gone, but democracy has not yet taken hold in all societies. More education is part of the answer.

Better education will provide job opportunities, remove prejudice, and create respect for life. I hope the time will come when individual merit will be more important than color, culture, language, or religion. We have come a long way in educated societies like the United States, where integration is happening fast, including interreligious marriages. Bhagat Kabir has a composition in the Guru Granth Sahib: *"Awwal Allah Noor Uppia, Kudret they sub bande ek noor te sub jag upje, kaun pale, kaun mande."* (All human beings are created equal by God. Nobody can claim to be superior or inferior.)

When I was a ten-year-old boy living happily with my family in Chattha Chak No. 46, I never anticipated the transformation that would come to me and to my land. Perhaps there will come a time when we will all become global citizens with no caste, creed, religion, color, or nationality.

Long live Punjab. Long live India. Long live the United States. Long live love.

. . . .

The world is my country, all mankind are my brethren, and to do good is my religion.

—Thomas Paine

. . . .

Acknowledgments

I must confess at the outset that I am not a journalist or writer; I am by profession a physician. However, I lived through Partition as a boy, and it is a topic I have discussed and explored with my wife and with my children as they grew. After I retired from years of practicing medicine, my family urged me to pen my boyhood experience to share it with others. I appreciate their support and encouragement to undertake this project.

Mine is not the only experience recounted here. Partition prompted a huge movement of population, and there are many stories to tell from that time. I have been fortunate to have two friends—Hardial Dhaliwal and Ajit Chattha—who shared their experiences with me and whose stories I include in this book. I also include the story of my cousin Mohinder, who, though young at the time of the migration, recounted to me her memories of that awful time. All four of us were quite young during the period of upheaval, and each of us has something unique to add to the collective memories of the experience. I am thankful to all of them for sharing their experience without concern for their privacy.

My children, Geetinder, Sonia, and Vijay; their respective spouses, Eldan Eichbaum, Harvinder Sandhu, and Archana Chattha; and my grandchildren, Yasmin, Anju, Josh, Alexi, Arjan, Rani, Amrik, Taj, and Jaia, were patient as I took time from their activities to work on this project. My nephew Darshan Chattha helped me to collect many Partition-related poems and photographs. My older cousin Harbhajan Singh Chattha helped me to recollect many names of Pakistani Chatthas.

This project would not have been possible without the support of the all-important person in my life, my life partner, Dr. Jaswinder K. Chattha. She and I met when we were students at medical college in Patiala, India, and were married during our last year there. We moved to the United States for further medical training and ended up staying. It was in America that we raised our three children. We are indebted to both our mother country, "Free India," and our chosen country, America.

I am grateful for the blessing of my role model and older brother S. Ajit S. Chattha, IAS. He supplied additional historical facts about events that occurred during Partition and also put me in touch with people who experienced the partition themselves. Ranbir Singh Bajwa was kind enough to give me a copy of a small booklet written by his father, Dr. Virsa Singh, recounting his eye-witness account of the attack on the village of Bhulair.

I personally did not do any archive searches and am thankful to authors Larry Collins and Dominique Lapierre, Yasmin Khan, Nisid Hajari, Urvashi Butalia, and Ishtiaq Ahmed for their informative books. I am especiallly thankful to Ishtiaq Ahmed for many insightful historical events pertaining to the great city of Lahore, the capital of combined Punjab, his birthplace, where such violence occured. He knew every nook and corner of the city. I am also grateful to

Paul Michael Taylor, PhD, director, Asian Cultural History Program, Smithsonian Institution; S. Tarlochan Singh, former chair of the National Commission for Minorities, India; Dr. B. S. Ghuman, vice chancellor, Punjabi University (Patiala); Harish Khare, journalist and former editor-in-chief of *The Tribune*: Punjab (India); Lady Kishwar Desai, chair of The Arts and Cultural Heritage Trust. They were kind enough to give their valuable comments and advice.

Amy Popplewell typed multiple revisions and helped to improve the manuscript. Jimmy "Love" Little designed the cover. The librarians at the Woodside Library and the Novato Library (in California) and Greenwich Library (in Connecticut) procured some rare books for me, for which I am grateful. And Andi Reese Brady, of Personal History Productions LLC, skillfully edited my manuscript.

Heather Chattha, my distant uncle from Pakistan, relayed to me the events that led up to my family's sudden departure from our village. He also arranged my trip to that village, Chattha Chak No. 46, now within Pakistan. Drs. Satinder and Tejinder Bhullar were instrumental in helping to arrange portions of that trip to Pakistan and, during the trip, took photographs of our historic journey, some of which I use in this book. Our Punjabi hosts—Nafisa Din, Nusrat Saeed, Saeed Iqbal, Mushtaq and Rukhsana Tahirkheli, and a few others in Pakistan—provided unmatched hospitality. I am sure I missed some names, for which I blame my memory. This undertaking was the combined effort of many, and I thank all who contributed.

Works Consulted

Ahmed, Ishtiaq. *The Punjab Bloodied, Partitioned and Cleansed: Unravelling the 1947 Tragedy through Secret British Reports and First-person Accounts.* Karachi: Oxford UP, 2012. Print.

Ali, Choudhry Rahmat. "Now or Never: Are We to Live or Perish Forever?" *Columbia University.* N.p., n.d. Web. 4 Dec. 2007.

Bajwa, Virsa Singh. Shahidi Saka Bhuler [*Patriotic Story of Bhuler*], Jan. 1948. Translated from Punjabi by Amrik Singh Chattha.

Bergland, Christopher. "The Neuroscience of Empathy." *Psychology Today.* Sussex Publishers, 10 Oct. 2013. Web. 27 June 2017.

Berreby, David. *Us and Them: The Science of Identity.* Chicago: 2008.

Bhagat, Kabir. *Guru Granth Sahib.* N.p.: n.p., n.d. 1349. Print.

Bon, Gustave Le, and Gabriel Tarde. *The Crowd: A Study of the Popular Mind.* N.p.: Project Gutenberg, 1895. Print.

Butalia, Urvashi. *The Other Side of Silence: Voices from the Partition of India.* Durham, NC: Duke U, 2000. Print.

Cikara M. et al. "Reduced Self-Referential Neural Response During Intergroup Competition Predicts Competitor Harm. *National Institutes of Health.* 1 Aug 2014. Web. 7 July 2017.

Coll, Steve. "The Back Channel." *The New Yorker*. The New Yorker, 20 June 2017. Web. 27 June 2017.

Collins, Larry, and Dominique Lapierre. *Freedom at Midnight: The Epic Drama of India's Struggle for Independence*. N.p.: Avon, 1975. Print.

Cronin, Brenda, and Rory Jones. "Elie Wiesel, Holocaust Survivor and Nobel Laureate, Dies at 87." *The Wall Street Journal*. Dow Jones & Company, 02 July 2016. Web. 28 June 2017.

Dalrymple, William. "The Mutual Genocide of Indian Partition." *The New Yorker*. The New Yorker, 19 June 2017. Web. 27 June 2017.

Dalrymple, William. *White Mughals: Love and Betrayal in Eighteenth-century India*. London: Penguin, 2004. Print.

Darling, Malcolm, and Ian Talbot. *At Freedom's Door*. Oxford: Oxford UP, 2011. Print.

Dias, Brian G. and Kerry J. Ressler. "Parental Olfactory Experience Influences Behavior and Neural Structure in Subsequent Generations." Nature Neuroscience. Vol 17, pp 89–96, 2014.

Frank, Anne. *The Diary of a Young Girl: Anne Frank*. Ed. Otto H. Frank and Mirjam Pressler. Trans. Susan Massotty. New York: Bantam, 1997. Print.

Gupta, Ashoka, and Amar Kumar Varma, Sudha Sen, Bina Das and Sheila Davar. "East Is East, West Is West. Seminar (510) special issue on "Porous Borders, Divided Selves." *India-seminar.com*. N.p., Feb. 2002. Web.

Hajari, Nisid. *Midnight's Furies: The Deadly Legacy of India's Partition*. N.p.: Houghton Mifflin Harcourt, 2015. Print.

Hitchens, Christopher. "The Perils of Partition." *The Atlantic*. Atlantic Media Company, 01 Mar. 2003. Web. 28 June 2017.

Hourani, Albert. *A History of the Arab Peoples*. Massachusetts: Harvard UP, 1991. Print.

Hughes, Virginia. "Mice Inherit Specific Memories, Because Epigenetics?" *National Geographic* blog "Only Human." 12 Dec 2013. Web. 20 July 2017.

India-seminar.com. New Delhi: Seminar Publications. Web. 28 January 2018.

"Islam and Modernity." *Wikipedia*. Wikimedia Foundation, 14 June 2017. Web. 28 June 2017.

Jaffrelot, Christophe. *Pakistan at the Crossroads: Domestic Dynamics and External Pressures*. New York: Columbia UP, 2016. Print.

Karthik, Venkatesh. "Revisiting Bhagat Singh's Idea of India." *Tribune (India*; Punjab). 22 March 2017, http://epaper.tribuneindia.com/c/17787716.

Kean, Hilda. *The Great Cat and Dog Massacre: The Real Story of World War Two's Unknown Tragedy*. Chicago: U of Chicago, 2017. Print.

Khan, Yasmin. *The Great Partition: The Making of India and Pakistan*. New Haven: Yale UP, 2007. Print.

K.T.S., Tulsi. "Silver Lining in the Clouds of Partition." *The Turbine Saturday*. N.p., 17 Apr. 1999. Web. 28 June 2017.

Kübler-Ross, Elisabeth, and David Kessler. *On Grief and Grieving: Finding the Meaning of Grief through the Five Stages of Loss*. New York: Scribner, 2014. Print.

Laskier, Rutka. *Rutka's Notebook: A Voice from the Holocaust*. New York: Time / Yad Vashem, 2008. Print.

Leeds, University of. "Sheep in Human Clothing - Scientists Reveal Our Flock Mentality." *Ext Temp 1*. Leeds, 16 Dec. 2009. Web. 28 June 2017.

Manto, Saadat Hasan. *Toba Tek Singh: Stories*. Trans. Francis W. Prichard. New Delhi: Penguin, 2011. Print.

Miczek, Klaus A., Rosa M. M. De Almeida, Edward A. Kravitz, Emilie F. Rissman, Sietse F. De Boer, and Adrian Raine. "Neurobiology of Escalated Aggression and Violence." *Journal of Neuroscience*.

Society for Neuroscience, 31 Oct. 2007. Web. 27 June 2017.

Moon, Penderel. *Divide and Quit*. London: Chatto and Windus, 1961. Print.

Moore, David S. *Developing Genome: An Introduction to Behavioral Epigenetics*. S.l.: Oxford UP, 2015. Print.

Mukherjee, Siddhartha. "The Science of Identity and Difference." *The New Yorker*. The New Yorker, 19 June 2017. Web. 28 June 2017.

Nayar, Kuldip, Asif Noorani, and David Page. *Tales of Two Cities*. N.p.: Lotus Roli, 2008. Print.

"Pandit Jawarharlal Nehru (1889–1964)." *Humanists UK*. N.p., 30 Aug. 2016. Web. 14 Mar. 2017.

Patel, Aakar. *The News* (op-ed). 22 Sept. 2008.

Pemment, Jack. "The Neurobiology of Antisocial Personality Disorder: The Quest for Rehabilitation and Treatment." *Elsevier*. N.p., 4 Oct. 2012. Web. 27 June 2017.

Pinker, Susan. "Charlie Hebdo and Religious Blinders." *Time*. Time, 13 Jan. 2015. Web. 27 June 2017.

Powledge, Tabitha. *Behavioral Epigenetics How Nurture Shapes Nature Bioscience*. Vol. 61. N.p.: n.p., 2011. 588–92. Print.

Raine, Adrian. *Anatomy of Violence: The Biological Roots of Crime*. New York: Vintage, 2014. Print.

Rukhshanda, Jalil, et al. *Looking Back: The 1947 Partition of India, 70 Years On*. Orient Blackswan, 2017.

Sapolsky, Robert M. "Mind and Matter." *Wall Street Journal*. N.p., 29 Apr. 2016. Web.

---. "Why Your Brain Hates Other People. *Nautilus*. 22 June 2017. Web. 15 June 2017.

Satia, Priya. "Poets of Partition." *Tanqeed*. N.p., Jan. 2016. Web. 28 June 2017.

Scott, Paul. *The Jewel in the Crown*. Chicago: U of Chicago, 1998. Print.

Sekhri, V. N. *A Lament: Was Partition Inescapable?* New Delhi: New Age, 2007. Print.

"Siege of Masada." *Wikipedia.* Wikimedia Foundation, 25 June 2017. Web. 27 June 2017.

Siever, Larry J. "Neurobiology of Aggression and Violence." *American Journal of Psychiatry.* Vol. 165, Issue 4, April 2008. Web 15 July 2017.

Singh, Amardeep. *Lost Heritage: The Sikh Legacy in Pakistan.* New Delhi: Nagaara Trust in Association with Himalayan, 2016. Print.

Soroush, Abdolkarim. "The Responsibility of the Muslim Intellectual in the 21st Century." Interview by Farish A. Noor. *Nawaat.* N.p., 30 Jan. 2005. Web. 28 June 2017.

Talbot, Ian and Gurharpal Singh. *The Partition of India.* N.p.: Cambridge UP, 2009.

Tamara, Avant. "Examining the Mob Mentality." *The Green Issue.* N.p., 1 Jan. 2011. Web. 28 June 2017.

"Tribune India The Tribune Epaper Dated Sat, 17 Oct 15." *The Tribune.* N.p., 17 Oct. 2016. Web. 28 June 2017.

Trotter, William. *Instincts of the Herd in Peace and War.* New York: Macmillan Collector's Library, 1915. Print.

Virk, Hardev Singh. *Professor Puran Singh: Scientist, Poet & Philosopher.* Chandigarh: Tarlochan, 2008. Print.

Waal, Frans de. *Are We Smart Enough To Know How Smart Animals Are?* New York: W. W. Norton, 2016. Print.

Yanowitch, Rachel, and Emil F. Coccaro. *The Neurochemistry of Human Aggression.* Vol. 75. N.p.: Advances in Genetics, 2011. 151-69. Print.

Zahir, M. *1947: A Memoir of Indian Independence.* Victoria, B.C.: Trafford, 2009. Print.

About the Author

Amrik Singh Chattha was born September 1, 1937, in Chattha Chak No. 46, now located in Pakistan. His educational journey took him, in India, through Sikh National College, Qadian; Government Medical College, Patiala (where he met his wife, also a medical student); and Government Medical College, Amritsar; and in the United States, from Drake Memorial Hospital, Cincinnati, Ohio; New York Medical College, New York City; to Boston Children's Hospital and Mass General Hospital, Boston, both affiliated with Harvard Medical School, where he was a fellow in neurology.

He spent five years in Boston training in neurology. He and his family then moved to Weirton, West Virginia, where he practiced neurology for forty-one years, finally retiring to the San Francisco Bay Area.

Since his marriage to Dr. Jaswinder Kaur Brar, in 1961, they have journeyed together.

Professional Organizations

American Academy of Neurology
Hancock County Medical Society, West Virginia
Jefferson County Medical Society, Ohio

Community Organizations

President, Sikh Council of North America, 1982

Founding member, Tristate Sikh Cultural Society (helped the building of the Sikh Gurdwara at Pittsburgh; organized Sikh youth camps)

Founding member of the alumni organization, Government Medical College, Patiala

Founding member, Patiala Health Foundation

Other

Member, Sikh Heritage Foundation, which created a Sikh exhibit at the Smithsonian (opened in 2004; now a traveling exhibit)

Sponsor of two books: *Sikh Heritage: Ethos & Relics* and *Sikhs: Legacy of the Punjab* (developed by the Smithsonian)

Endowed a chair in Sikh Studies at the University of Michigan (the chair is named in honor of parents, Tara Singh and Balwant Kaur Chattha, and Gurbaksh Singh and Kirpal Kaur Brar)

Amrik Singh Chattha and Jaswinder Kaur Chattha, 2017

Index

Ali Sardar Jafri (poet), 120

Alipur chatha, 3

Alvi, Moniza (poet), 120

Amardeep Singh, 141

Amrik Singh Chattha

and Ajit Singh Chattha (friend), 80–83

ancestors and descendents of, 5

childhood days, 12–13

examples of mutual love among Punjabis, 129–130

family, 3–13

first encounter with British and bribery, 19–21, 69

grandfather's family, 6

and Gulam Heather Chattha, 125–129

with his Muslim kin (Chattha Chak No. 46), 132

and independence, 25–26

and Jaswinder K. Chattha (spouse), 128, 131–135, 142, 202

key locations in Punjab during his journeys, xv

met Giani Kartar Singh, 38

and Mohinder (cousin sister), 84–86

at National Mosque, in Islamabad, 132

Sardarni Balwant Kaur (mother), 12

schooling in India, 68–69

Tara Singh Chattha (father), 6, 10–12

trip to Pakistan, pilgrimage to his birthplace, 131–145

visiting Pakistan, in 1997, 128, 129

Wadhawa Singh (grandfather), 4–10

Amrita Pritam (poet), 49, 103, 110–111, 168

Amritsar, 66

amygdala, 155–156

animals

Khalsa, 4

Khushwant Singh (writer), 168

Kipling, Rudyard, 166

Kuldip Nayar (journalist), 168

Laggi Nazr punjab nu (poem), 177–178

language, 137–138

life in camps, 95–97

Looking Back: The 1947 Partition of India, 70 Years On (book), 119

loss

    of loved ones, 121

    material, 121

    psychological/emotional, 122

Lost Heritage: The Sikh Legacy in Pakistan (book), 141–142

love and hatred, 163

mahants (hereditary managers of Gurdwaras), 15

Maharaj Singh, 32

mahashas people, 97

Man Singh Parwana, 84

Manjit Singh Chattha, 125–126

Manmohan Singh, 168

Mannes, Marya (poet), 120

Manto, Saadat Hasan, 102

marriage, 139

Masada fortress, in Israel, 56

material loss, 121

Maulana Azad, 22, 35, 36, *37*, 42

meat, 138

media, 24